On
Desert Trails
with
Everett Ruess

Everett Ruess and his dog, Curly.

On
Desert Trails
with
Everett Ruess

Commemorative Edition

With an Introduction by Hugh Lacy
and a Foreword by Randall Henderson, Editor, *Desert Magazine*

Edited and with an Afterword by Gary James Bergera
Epilogue by W. L. Rusho

GIBBS·SMITH PUBLISHER

SALT LAKE CITY

04 03 02 01 00   5 4 3 2 1

Published by
Gibbs Smith, Publisher
P.O. Box 667
Layton, Utah 84041

Orders: (1-800) 748-5439
Website: *www.gibbs-smith.com*

Edited by Linda Nimori
Cover design by Derek Lancaster
Interior design and book production by Ray Cornia
Printed and bound in the USA

Library of Congress Cataloging-in-Publication Data

Ruess, Everett, b. 1914.
    On desert trails with Everett Ruess. – Commemorative ed. / edited by Gary James Bergera.
        p. cm.
    Originally published: El Centro, Calif. : Desert Magazine Press, 1940.
    ISBN 0-87905-825-0
    1. Ruess, Everett, b. 1914—Correspondence. 2. Ruess, Everett, b. 1914—Homes and haunts—Southwest, New. 3. Poets,
American—20th century—Correspondence. 4. Explorers—Southwest, New—Correspondence. 5. Southwest, New—
Description and travel. 6. Artists—Southwest, New—Correspondence. 7. Southwest, New—Poetry. I. Bergera, Gary James.
II. Title.
    PS3535.U26Z48   2000
    811'.52—dc21
    [B]   97-19945
                                                                                                              CIP

Contents

Editor's Preface to the Commemorative Edition vii

Foreword by Randall Henderson ix

"Son!" by Stella Knight Ruess x

"Say That I Kept My Dream" by Hugh Lacy xi

Where Everett Ruess Vanished xiv

Poems and Letters by Everett Ruess 1

    Poems · 1929 2
        The Relic — 2
        Two Arrowheads — 2
        The Indian Council Cave — 3
        Pledge to the Wind — 4

    Poems · 1930 5
        Life Is a Song — 5
        Colors I've Failed to Catch — 5
        My Life Shall Be a Little Curling Wave — 6
        My Soul Set Free — 7

    Letters · 1931 8
        I Have Really Lived — 8
        I Shall Take the Trail Again — 9
        Pegasus Folded His Wings — 10
        Dance of the Tumbleweeds — 11
        I'm Willing to Pay — 12
        I Shall Be Drifting South — 13
        Sunset Made the Misery Worth Enduring — 14
        I Am Not a Haggler — 15
        Idyllic Days Watching the Clouds Go By — 16
        Spirit of the Wilderness Trail — 17

    Letters · 1932 18
        The Willow Trees Bend Low — 18
        The Lone Trail Is Best for Me — 19
        Tragedy in the Canyon of Death — 19
        Exploring the Indian Ruins — 21
        I Go to Make My Destiny — 23
        Wilderness Journeys of 1932 — 24

    Letters and Poems · 1933 27
        I Am Going to Shoulder My Pack — 27
        Fragments — 28
        It Is Always Time to Live — 28
        I Have Lived Intensely — 29
        Over Unknown Canyon Trails by Moonlight — 30
        I Had a Delightful Trip to Siberian Pass — 31
        All Is a Golden Dream — 31

Everett's Quiz from the Desert — 32
Wilderness Song — 33

Letters · 1934 34
    I Do Not Regret My Freedom — 34
    What I Most Wanted to Do — 34
    I Had a Strange Ride Last Night — 35
    I Had to Make a Painting — 36
    The Burros Bolted into the Night — 37
    I Shall Always Be a Rover — 38
    I Have Been Flirting with Death — 39
    I Stayed with the Navajo — 40
    When I Go I Leave No Trace — 42
    Camp at Navajo Mountain — 44
    Here I Am Truly Alone — 45
    Excavating at Basket Maker Cave — 46
    I Almost Lost One Burro — 48
    At the Hopi Ceremonial Dance — 49
    I Danced with the Hopi — 49
    I Drove Away Evil Spirits — 50
    Heading Across the Pink Cliffs — 51
    Tomorrow I Take the Trail Again — 52
    I Have Not Tired of the Wilderness — 53

"What Became of Everett Ruess" by Hugh Lacy 54

Appendix 59
    "Is Everett Ruess in Mexico?" by Cora L. Keagle — 60
    Letter from Tad Nichols — 61
    "Who Was 'Nemo'?" by Christopher G. Ruess — 62
    Letter from Lawrence Janssens — 63
    "Everett's Home" by Randall Henderson — 64
    Everett Ruess Awards — 66

    Three Poems and Six Letters by Everett Ruess,
    Previously Unpublished, from "Youth Is for Adventure" — 67

    The *Salt Lake Tribune*'s Account of Its 1935 Expedition
    to Southern Utah in Search of Everett Ruess — 74

    "In Search of an Old Inscription: Utah Trip 1935" by Stella Knight Ruess — 94

Epilogue by W. L. Rusho 98
    "Everett Ruess and His Footprints"

Afterword by Gary James Bergera 106
    " 'The Murderous Pain of Living': Thoughts on the Death of Everett Ruess"

Endnotes 118

Bibliography 128

List of Illustrations 129

Editor's Preface to the Commemorative Edition

During the two years following Everett Ruess's disappearance in southern Utah in November 1934, his parents, Christopher and Stella Knight Ruess (pronounced Rooess), edited a collection of his diaries, essays, poetry, letters, photographs, blockprints, and paintings. Entitled "Youth Is for Adventure," this 277-page compilation was dedicated to "Lovers of Nature, of Music, of Beauty." In view of the attention generated by Everett's disappearance and subsequent publication of a few of his letters, they hoped to interest a national publisher in their son's life and in the mystery surrounding his presumed death. As they explained in their preface, dated 28 March 1937, Everett's twenty-third birthday,

> *Many readers today are deeply interested in psychology and psychiatry. They will discover much in the lines and between the lines. Here are hinted the conflicts, yearnings and queries of a youth highly sensitive to nature, to music and to beauty. He begrudged the time and energy our economic system exacts of artist, artisan and laborer alike. At times Everett believed that art and artists should be subsidized. At other times he felt that the battle makes the man.*
>
> *It may be that many will take this little volume along on vacation wanderings, especially in the California Parks and the High Sierras and in the great Southwest. Others in dreary rooms and lonesome hotels in rancous cities will find that it recreates the peace of the pines and of the sequoias and the quiet of starry nights by little lakes, and that it brings balm for the harassed spirit.*

Included in "Youth Is for Adventure" were the following materials: eight photographs "by and of Everett"; some twenty blockprints "chiefly by Everett"; at least nine watercolors "by Everett"; excerpts from Everett's diary of "Sequoia–Mt. Whitney–Yosemite Wanderings, 1933"; excerpts from Everett's diary of "The Southwestern Deseret—Arizona, New Mexico, Colorado, 1932"; thirteen "Poems, 1928–1933"; fifteen "Essays, 1926–1933," mostly from high school and college; fifty-three letters, in excerpts or in their entirety, dated 1930–34; Stella Ruess's poem "Son"; and an index. Although the Ruesses were unable to interest a major publisher, their work served as a basis for the excerpts *Desert Magazine* published in 1939 and then reissued the following year in expanded form as *On Desert Trails with Everett Ruess* (El Centro, California: Desert Magazine Press). A second edition—redesigned, reset, rearranged, retitled, and some of the contents dropped—appeared in 1950 (Palm Desert, California: Desert Magazine Press).

In preparing Everett's writings for publication, first in "Youth Is for Adventure" and then in *Desert Magazine* and *On Desert Trails*, the Ruesses tried to faithfully reproduce Everett's words as he wrote them. However, they tended to standardize spelling, capitalization, and grammar, as well as deleted some text from the material they chose to print. Fortunately, most of these omissions were later restored in W. L. Rusho's *Everett Ruess: A Vagabond for Beauty* (Salt Lake City: Peregrine Smith Books, Gibbs Smith, Publisher, 1983). A few sentences, paragraphs, and letters, however, remain unpublished.

This new commemorative edition of *On Desert Trails* differs from the first edition in the following ways:

1. It begins with a new table of contents and this editor's preface, and deletes the original table of contents, the original pencil sketches by Norton Allen (except his map) and by G. A. Randall, the original index, and the poem by Jean Baker, "Youth Is for Adventure." The illustrations were selected and captioned by the publisher.

2. It arranges the letters, poems, etc., in more or less chronological order.

3. It compares the texts of the letters, poems, etc., against their appearance(s) in the *Salt Lake Tribune*, "Youth Is for Adventure," *Desert Magazine, A Vagabond for Beauty*, and elsewhere, as well as against the original manuscripts when possible. While most omissions are identified with bracketed ellipses, and other occasional, possibly significant differences are noted, no attempt has been made to present a line-by-line comparison. All endnotes are the current editor's.

4. It silently corrects a handful of obvious typographical errors.

5. It inserts into the main text excerpts from two letters that originally appeared in "Everett's Home," by Randall Henderson, at the conclusion to *On Desert Trails* (where they still appear in this reprint edition).

6. It features a new epilogue by Ruess scholar W. L. Rusho, entitled "Everett Ruess and His Footprints," and an editor's afterword, entitled "'The Murderous Pain of Living': Thoughts on the Death of Everett Ruess."

7. And it contains three new appendices: three poems and six letters by Everett, previously unpublished, taken from "Youth Is for Adventure"; the *Salt Lake Tribune*'s account of its 1935 expedition to southern Utah in search of Everett following his disappearance; and Stella Ruess's "In Search of an Old Inscription: Utah Trip 1935," previously unpublished.

Other than these changes, the text remains as it appeared in *On Desert Trails* and includes eight poems ("Son!" [by his mother], "The Relic," "Two Arrowheads," "My Life Shall Be a Little Curling Wave," "Colors I've Failed to Catch," "Life Is a Song," "My Soul Set Free," and "Fragments") and six letters ("Idyllic Days Watching the Clouds Go By," "Wilderness Journeys of 1932," "I Had a Delightful Trip to Siberian Pass," "I Had a Strange Ride Last Night," "The Burros Bolted into the Night," and "I Almost Lost One Burro"), as well as three previously unpublished poems ("Morning in Los Angeles Harbor," "The Air Circus," and "The Ballad of the Lonely Skyscraper") and six previously unpublished letters ("Point Lobos," "Program of the 1931 Artists and Adventurers' Expedition," "My Little Month-old Puppy, Curly," "On the Crest of the Wave Again," "The Fiery Elixir of Beauty," and "I Have Been Enjoying the City") available nowhere else.

For their encouragement and assistance, I thank Lavina Fielding Anderson, Robert D. Anderson, Madge Baird, Jeffrey E. Keller, Stanford Layton, Mark Malcolm, Linda Nimori, Diane Orr, Ron Priddis, David Roberts, Kristen Rogers, Ken Sanders, Melissa Sanders, Gibbs Smith, Paul VanDenBerghe, Ken Verdoia, Kent Walgren, and especially W. L. Rusho, whose insights and cooperation proved particularly helpful.

—Gary James Bergera

Foreword

Everett Ruess, youthful artist and poet, was a vagabond of the remote Southwestern trails during a considerable part of four years. Then in November, 1934, he vanished in the desert wilderness of southern Utah. Later, searching parties found his burros in an isolated canyon. But to this day no clue has been discovered to explain his disappearance.

But while the fate of Everett remains a mystery, the dream which impelled him to forsake civilization for the solitude of remote canyons and arid plateaus, has been preserved in his paintings and verses, and in his frequent letters to family and friends.

Through collaboration with his parents, Stella and Christopher Ruess of Los Angeles, and Hugh Lacy, writer and friend of the Ruess family, the *Desert Magazine* published many of these letters serially during 1939.[1]

During the ensuing months there developed a widespread interest in the life and character of this young artist. Here was a youth who had visioned a new way of life—and deliberately turned his back on a good home and the conventional pursuits of young men of his age, to go out alone into the desert to travel and paint and write in the freedom of natural surroundings. It was not an easy existence he sought. On the contrary it was a life of deprivation and hazard. It was an existence that all imaginative persons dream about—but that few have the will and courage to achieve.

Readers of the Desert Magazine—literally hundreds of them—wrote letters to the publishing office. They wanted to know more about Everett Ruess. Some of them volunteered to renew the search for him. Since it was impracticable to publish all the material serially, Mr. and Mrs. Ruess agreed to the suggestion that a more complete record of Everett's desert wanderings be compiled in book form. Hence this volume.

It is offered, not merely as entertainment, but as an intimate picture of a very intelligent young man who sought in his own way to find the solution to some of the most difficult of the problems which confront all human beings in this highly complex age. We cannot all be wanderers, nor writers nor painters. But from the philosophy of Everett Ruess we may all draw something that will contribute to our understanding of the basic values of the universe in which we live.

Everett Ruess, to an unusual degree, had the ability to translate in vivid words the beauties of his everyday environment in the great outdoors. His was the soul of a true artist—but an artist who clung tenaciously to the realities of life, and therein lies the secret of the far-reaching response his words inevitably find in the hearts of those who read his story.

—Randall Henderson
[1940]

Everett and Curly, relaxing at home in Los Angeles, 1931.

Son! [2]

Somewhere your eyes light up to beauty near or far;
Somewhere your spirit lives where kindred spirits are.
Along the paths of loneliness your feet, rough-shod,
Through canyons dark and steep and treacherous have trod.
Across the windy desert-stretch you found your way,
An Indian hogan sheltered you at close of day.
Up winding, rugged trails you eagerly have gone
To watch the mystery of stars and vibrant dawn.
Brave storm-tossed trees companioned you, bright wayside
      flowers,
Faint tinkle of the burro-bells, bold granite towers,
Remembered melodies, and chanted poetry.
Somehow your thoughts are winging through the clouds to me.

           —by Stella Knight Ruess, Everett's Mother

"Say That I Kept My Dream ..." [3]
by Hugh Lacy

Wherever poets, adventurers and wanderers of the Southwest gather, the story of Everett Ruess will be told. His name, like woodsmoke, conjures far horizons.

Everett left Kayenta, Arizona, November 11, 1934, to write, paint and explore among a group of ancient Indian cliff dwellings. His last letter to his parents in Los Angeles explained that he would be unable to communicate for ten weeks.[4] Alone with his paints, books and two burros, he disappeared into what is probably the most uninhabited, unvisited section of the United States.

He never came back.

A sheepherder reported seeing him on November 19 near where Escalante creek flows into the Colorado.

At the first alarm of his prolonged absence, volunteers organized searching parties, combed the hills and canyons for days. Signal fires were built, guns fired. Indians and scouts sought water holes for signs of his passing.

In Davis canyon Everett's two burros were located, contentedly grazing as if he had just left them expecting shortly to return.

Then, one after another, the searching parties returned without Everett. True to his camping creed, "When I go, I leave no trace," he vanished—into thin air.

The desert claimed Everett Ruess. Writer, adventurer and artist, the desert's trails were his roads to romance. His paintings captured the black-shadowed desolation of cliff dwellings. His poetry told of wind and cliff ledge. He sang of the wasteland's moods. Everett belonged to the desert. And in the end, it claimed him.

He was one of the earth's oddlings—one of the wandering few who deny restraint and scorn inhibition. His life was a quest for the new and the fresh. Beauty was a dream. He pursued his dream into desert solitudes—there with the singing wind to chant his final song.

Everett's quest began early—and ended early. As a child he turned from toys to explore color and rhyme. Woodcarving, claymodeling and sketching occupied his formative years in New York and near Chicago. From this early background grew his versatility in the arts—media through which he later interpreted the multihued desert.

At 12 Everett found his element—writing. He wrote inquiring essays, haunting verse; he began a literary diary. The diary matured into travel-worn, adventure-laden tomes. Wind and rain added marks to the penciled pages, scrawled by the light of many campfires.

At 15 Everett was a member of Mrs. Snow Longley Housh's 1929 creative poetry class at the Los Angeles High School. An earlier spur to verse writing occurred with his winning Mrs. Margarette Ball Dickson's book, "Tumbleweeds," as an award for his Indian poem, "The Relic," written while a student at Valparaiso High School, Indiana. The silence of wilderness nights during his desert vagabondage was broken by his chant of remembered songs—poems that (in his diaries) he stated lifted his spirits and renewed his courage.

Even in early years the wild called Everett. The ocean's restlessness matched his own; mountains lured him; the desert fascinated him. His poems were of space, wind, sand, and sage.

And then, at 18 his hope-dream of distance crystallized. He wrote his last boyish essay. In part—

"One night, long ago, while I tossed restlessly upon my bed, an idea crystallized within me . . . My brain was busied with tense imaginings . . . In my mind I conjured up a thousand forgotten cities, left behind by the years; sheer grey mountains; mile upon mile of bare, unfriendly desert; cold lakes . . . jungles filled with deadly snakes, immense butterflies, brilliant colors, fever and death. I swam in coral-tinted waters. Through insufferable heat and incessant downpours I plodded forward.

"On bleak, windswept coasts . . . I pitched my camps. On the banks of the sluggish Amazon I built my fires . . . I tramped alone through wildernesses . . . On storm-lashed islands I stood, surveying far-off mountain peaks. Then I camped beneath them in shadowed valleys, watching the sunset . . . These are the things I saw and the experiences I lived through that night long past. Now it is night again—the night before I go. Once more I think of that which lies ahead.

"Bitter pain is in store for me, but I shall bear it. Beauty beyond all power to convey shall be mine . . . Death may await me . . . Not through cynicism and ennui will I be easy prey. And regardless of all that may befall, let me not be found to lack an understanding of the inscrutable humor of it all."

That was Everett's farewell to boyhood and home.

He journeyed by horse and burro in Arizona, New Mexico, Utah, and Colorado during 1931, '32 and '34. Through the summers of '30 and '33 he trekked the length and breadth of Sequoia and Yosemite Parks and the High Sierra. As he wandered he sang remembered themes from the great operas and symphonies. He read, wrote, painted and thought, and was formulating a philosophy to meet the exigencies of his artist-vagabond existence.

Everett's last letter to his brother, Waldo, said, ". . . as to when I revisit civilization, it will not be soon. I have not tired of the wilderness . . . I prefer the saddle to the street car, and the star-sprinkled sky to the roof, the obscure and difficult leading into the unknown . . . It is enough that I am surrounded with beauty . . . This has been a full, rich year. I have left no strange or delightful thing undone that I wanted to do."

In Arizona he rode broncos, branded calves and explored cliff dwellings, where, as he wrote, "The dim and silent centuries invade." In 1934 he worked with University of California archaeologists excavating near Kayenta. He was the only white man to be painted that year by the Hopis for their traditional Antelope Dance. He spoke Navajo and sang Indian songs. Once with a painted brave he chanted prayer-songs at the bedside of a sick Indian girl.

As he traveled he sold or traded blockprints and watercolors.

He endured stoically—like a good Indian—the hardships of his lonely life.

Among the earth's wastelands he found nepenthe for what he termed "an undercurrent of restlessness and wild longing." He often said, "I, too, long for that inner stillness, but I have yet more of the wild songs of youth to sing."

Alone in an immensity of drifting sand and fingerlike peaks, Everett forgot the passage of time. He forgot that civilization awaited his return. Everett forgot all but the mystery-laden voice of the wind, promising to reveal to him the secrecies of distance. Here was the beauty he sought. He absorbed the mauve and pastel splendor, climbed cliffs, explored, forgetting to return . . .

So far as is known, Everett did not live to see his 21st birthday, March 28, 1935. Numerous theories fail to explain his disappearance. Only the wind to which he was pledged (at 15 he wrote the poem, "I Have Given the Wind My Pledge") knows the answer to the riddle.

Strangely prophetic, these lines from his "Wilderness Song":

"Say that I starved; that I was lost and weary;
That I was burned and blinded by the desert sun;
Footsore, thirsty, sick with strange diseases;
Lonely and wet and cold, but that I kept my dream!"

A small insurance policy on Everett's life has been turned into an annuity. Each year, while his parents live, boys and girls of the southwestern states that Everett traversed will be invited to compete for honors in the arts he loved. So in his silence he will live on creatively.

His parents express the hope that more mothers and fathers may establish similar living memorials to sons and daughters whose life songs break after a stanza.

As to Everett. He kept his dream!

On and On and On!

Where Everett Ruess Vanished...

Everett Ruess departed from Escalante, Utah, November 12, 1934, for an indefinite trek through the uninhabited wilderness of southern Utah. Four months later, searchers found his two burros in a natural corral at the bottom of Davis canyon. The boy's footprints were discovered in a nearby cave. But no trace of Everett or his camping outfit has ever been disclosed. This map, drawn by Norton Allen of the Desert Magazine staff, shows the area where the search was made for the missing boy.

Poems and Letters

by Everett Ruess

Poems · 1929

The Relic

In a deserted field I found an arrowhead,
      Worn by the rains and snows of many a year.
It had survived its maker buried here,
For he who shot the arrow from his bow was dead.

How far this chiseled piece of flint leads back the mind!
      By careful Indian craftsman it was wrought,
To tip an arrow, held to bowstring taut,—
To me it was a very precious treasure-find.

          —by Everett Ruess, 1927[5]

Two Arrowheads

Today I found a faulty arrowhead,
      Rejected as unfitted for its work,
Its blunt point was never dyed with red
      From clotted blood. Where mountain lions lurk,
Its raking barbs ne'er tore a savage heart.
      Begun but never finished, crude and rough,
A flaw defied the Indian craftsman's art—
      His patience and his skill were not enough.

From finely chipped and faultless needle tip
      To well-proportioned barbs and spreading base,
The maker fashioned this without a slip—
      A point of flawless symmetry and grace.
Two arrowheads—one, never stained by strife;
The other, made and used to take a life.

          —by Everett Ruess, 1929

The Indian Council Cave[6]

Wand'ring among the painted rocks one day,
  I saw some ancient, moss-grown boulders there.
That leaned together in a friendly way,
  And formed a cave that might have housed a bear.
But on the high-arched ceiling were designs
  And symbols that some Indian had drawn,—
A rising sun, marked out in faint red lines,
  A row of running wolves, a deer and fawn.
Bones from forgotten feasts were on the floor,
  Picked clean by men who sat around a fire,
Discussing and deciding peace or war,
  Or dancing solemnly in gay attire.[7]
The cave is empty now; the paintings fade.
The dim and silent centuries invade.[8]

—published in "The American Indian," April, 1929

Granite Towers

Pledge to the Wind [9]

Onward from vast uncharted spaces,
      Forward through timeless voids,
Into all of us surges and races
      The measureless might of the wind.

Strongly sweeping from open plains,
      Keen and pure from mountain heights,
Freshly blowing after rains,
      It welds itself into our souls.

In the steep silence of thin blue air,
      High on a lonely cliff-ledge,
Where the air has a clear, clean rarity,
      I give to the wind . . . my pledge:

"By the strength of my arm, by the sight of my eyes,
      By the skill of my fingers, I swear,
As long as life dwells in me, never will I
      Follow any way but the sweeping way of the wind.

"I will feel the wind's buoyancy until I die;
      I will work with the wind's exhilaration;
I will search for its purity; and never will I
      Follow any way but the sweeping way of the wind."

Here in the utter stillness,
      High on a lonely cliff-ledge,
Where the air is trembling with lightning,
      I have given the wind my pledge.

—by Everett Ruess, 1929

Poems • 1930

Life Is a Song

Life is a song, and a happy one,
　　Else it would not be given us.
Let us not spoil it with drab and dun,
　　Why should we mar it with fret and fuss?

Life is a song, and a merry one,
　　Fill it with fun, and with lilting rhyme;
While it away with a laugh and a pun,
　　For gloom and the blues we have no time,

Life is a song, and a joyful one,
　　Dance it along to the very full.
Make it alight with the shining sun.
　　Live it along without a lull.

Life is happy, life is young;
Life should be glad from the bottom rung.
Life is merry, life is fast;
Life should be joy to the very last.

—by Everett Ruess, 1930[10]

Colors I've Failed to Catch

I only live to see again.
　　To mix and match
My colors to the visioned splendors
　　I've failed to catch.

—by Everett Ruess, 1930

My Life Shall Be a Little Curling Wave

My life shall be a little curling wave
     Gaily racing forth from the great blue sea.
A moment it will sparkle in the sun;
     Jewelled and scintillating it will flash,
Then with a little tinkling tune
     It will shatter on the cool brown sand
And turn to bubbling, milk white foam.
     So, broken, slowly it will retreat,
Leaving the beach a little smoother
     For the other waves that come.

—by Everett Ruess, 1930

Sea Spire

My Soul Set Free

Swirling madly through the winds of space
    My soul hurls onward to the distant sea,
And swooping from the mist and tattered clouds,
    It sings in wild delight, for it is free.

Far over firs and twisted mountain pines,
    Above the jagged, snowswept peaks it soars,
Then rends the granite with its smoking speed,
    While through the rock-ribbed crags it twirls and bores.

The flame gods follow from the riven cliff;
    My soul dives down and plunges in the lake
That lies below, to quench pursuing fires;
    Behind, it churns a foaming silver wake.

Then with torrential force it leaps to meet
    The sky, in one huge fountain spout of spray.
Exultantly it darts to find the sun,
    And mounts upon a glinting ray.

Then, shaking sunlight from its supple form,
    Again it takes a dive both long and steep
Until it cuts the ocean's welter, while
    The sparkling, crested breakers heave and leap.

Where seagull shadows fall across the waves,
    And high above, the sky is blue and wide,
Content, my soul drifts out alone to sea,
    Upon the surging, restless, rhythmic tide.

—by Everett Ruess, 1930

Letters • 1931

I Have Really Lived . . . [11]

Letter from Kayenta, Arizona, to his friend Bill Jacobs, April 18, 1931

Dear Bill:

As for my life, it is working out rather fortunately. These days away from the city have been the happiest of my life. It has all been a beautiful dream, sometimes tranquil, sometimes fantastic, and with enough pain and tragedy to make the delights possible by contrast. [. . .] The whole dream has been filled with warm and cool but perfect colors, and with aesthetic contemplation as I have jogged behind my little burro. A love for everyone and for everything has welled up, finding no outlet except in my art.

Music has been in my heart all the time, and poetry in my thoughts. Alone on the open desert, I have made up songs of wild, poignant rejoicing and transcendent melancholy. The world has seemed more beautiful to me than ever before. I have loved the red rocks, the twisted trees, the red sand blowing in the wind, the slow sunny clouds crossing the sky, the shafts of moonlight on my bed at night. I have seemed to be at one with the world. I have rejoiced to set out, to be going somewhere, and I have felt a still sublimity, looking [. . .] into the coals of my campfires, and seeing far beyond them. I have been happy in my work, and I have exulted in my play. I have really lived. [. . .]

In the meantime, my burro and I, and a little dog, if I can find one, are going on and on, until, sooner or later, we reach the end of the horizon.

Your alter ego,
LAN

[Note: "Lan" was a pen name often used by Everett.[12]]

Everett and friends, preparing to "take the trail again in a few days."

I Shall Take the Trail Again . . . [13]

Letter to Everett's brother Waldo from Kayenta, Arizona, April 19, 1931

Dear Waldo:

[. . .] Among the things in the three packages which I sent are: an ancient black and white Indian bowl; a modern black bowl, made by the Pueblo Indians; a mother of pearl ornament of value which I found at Keet Seel; a part of a human jawbone with teeth; some corn more than twelve hundred years old; and many types of pottery chips.

[. . .] But now to tell you of the real news. My family group has been enlarged to three! The latest is just following an ant across the hogan floor, in an attempt to find out what it is. Now he is chewing a scrap of rope as if it were a wild beast attacking him. He is a little roly-poly puppy with fluffy white fur, and blue brown patches on his head and near his tail. His eyes are blue and his nose is short. I found him last night, lost and squealing for help. When I stroked his fur in the darkness, electric sparks flew off.

I haven't yet decided about his name, but may call him Curly, because of his tail. When he is large enough, I am going to train him to go behind the burro, occasionally nipping the donkey's heels, so that we shall be able to go faster. It is quite amusing to see him sniffing and digging and investigating the world.

[. . .] I shall take the trail again in a few days. Repassing Kayenta, after ten days, I shall collect what mail there is and then strike out for Canyon de Chelly, returning westward through the Hopi reservation to the Grand Canyon, then north to Kaibab and Zion.

It is unfortunate that you have been unable to find a good position. No doubt your forty dollars savings has gone long ago. But you are probably enjoying life anyhow, even though you do not live it to the full. Nevertheless, when we read of the immense strides in accomplishment that some men have made in their youth, our own years often seem wasted. However, it is man's lot to be imperfect and discontented. In my travels in Arizona I have never met anyone whose life I envied. I myself feel much freer and happier here than I did in the city, but that is due not only to a change in environment, but to a change in my mental attitude.

My little family is a peaceful one. The puppy is taking a nap and the burro is eating sagebrush in a nearby field. The air is clear, fleecy clouds float dreamily overhead, and not a sound is to be heard anywhere, except the scratching of my pencil. I trust no unpleasant misadventures have befallen at home, and that you are not too much dissatisfied with the careless treatment of circumstance.

LOVE FROM LAN

Pegasus Folded His Wings... [14]

Letter to his family from Chin Lee,[15] Arizona, May 10, 1931

Dear Father, Mother and Waldo:

After four days travel, I arrived in Chin Lee from Kayenta. The distance was about 80 miles. One day I covered 25 miles, but towards afternoon, Pegasus[16] folded his wings, and progress was slow.

I contrived a roundelay, but found no one to sing it with:

> Prod, prod, prod, your burro
>   Gently near the tail,
> Merrily, merrily, merrily, merrily,
>   He's a kind of snail.

There has been much lightning, thunder, and rain. Once two rainbows appeared simultaneously. I watched until they vanished.

[. . .] I wish you would send a dozen copies apiece of my blockprints, Sky Seekers and The Rock and the Wave, in black and white, to give away. Also two or three of The Skyscraper.

Love from Everett

Sky Seekers

Dance of the Tumbleweeds... [17]

Letter to his family from near Flagstaff, Arizona, June 8, 1931

Dear Mother, Father and Waldo:

This letter is being sent from the vicinity of Flagstaff, not Grand Canyon. Yesterday noon I was at the Little Colorado river, about to turn westward, when along came two boys in a small Ford truck who were much interested in what I was doing. They had passed me near Hotevilla pueblo. One of them suddenly decided to take me and the burro and Curly to his ranch in the Coconino forest, among the San Francisco peaks. I was much surprised, and I did not consider the project feasible, but he was confident it could be done.

The three of us finally shunted the donkey on, after much maneuvering. The rest of the pack was lashed on the roof. Pegasus stumbled and lurched from side to side, but maintained his equilibrium. We sailed along through desert and forest, with the shadow of the donkey behind us. At dusk we reached their school, which has five teachers and five pupils. This afternoon I'll go to the ranch, and stay in the vicinity for a week or more. I expect to do some good painting and work out some blockprints. The mountain slope is covered with aspens, and wild life is very abundant. One of the boys, Rudolph Jenks,[18] is interested in ornithology. He wants to buy my painting of a cliff dwelling. [. . .]

So for a time I have left the heat of the desert behind me. The air is cool and bracing. It will be three or four thousand feet higher at the ranch.

[. . .] The pueblo of Walpi was rather a disillusionment. There is an element of incongruity in the juxtaposition of old stonework and fences made of bedsteads. [. . .]

I also passed through Toreva, Chimopovi, Old Oraibi, and Hotevilla. The dust and heat were extreme. When I was nearly at Blue Canyon, a young couple passed by, and saying that the canyon was dry, they gave me a gallon of water. I found that they were mistaken, and in a pocket in the rocks, I discovered an excellent swimming pool, of cool, green, shadowed water, with high rock walls. It was very deep too. Curly went swimming. I was startled to see what a tiny creature he is with fur wet down. Half of his size is fur. He enjoyed greatly the puppy biscuits you sent.[19] Everyone seems to love him.

The next day I saw a weird thing, the dance of the tumbleweeds. A small whirlwind picked them up and tossed them in large circles. They would float to earth and then bounce up again. Around and around they went in fantastic spirals.

On the following day I went through Moenkopi Village, another Hopi town. There were cliffs of bright vermilion, and the finest specimens of Lombardy poplars that I have ever seen. A scorpion started to crawl into my blankets, but I stopped him in time.

The next day[20] I paused by a stream to let the burros rest. Some Indians passed by me in a covered wagon, drawn by six horses and mules. The following two days were spent in the Painted Desert, until I reached the Little Colorado. I had walked [about] one hundred and seventy miles from Chin Lee.

Love from Everett

I'm Willing to Pay...[21]

Letter to Bill Jacobs from Zion Park, Utah, August, 1931[22]

Dear Bill:

For six days I've been suffering from my semi-annual poison ivy—my sufferings are far from over. For two days I couldn't tell whether I was dead or alive. I writhed and twisted in the heat, with swarms of ants and flies crawling over me, while the poison oozed and crusted on my face and arms and back. I ate nothing—there was nothing to do but suffer philosophically.

Yesterday I managed to pry my lips far enough apart to insert food. I thought my eyes would swell shut, but not so. Even now, they are mere slits in the puffed flesh. Nothing I used in times past alleviated the raging perceptibly.

[. . .] I get it every time, but I refuse to be driven out of the woods. My face is on fire as I write and my back has not reached the crisis yet, but if a few annual doses, however searing, are the price I must pay for doing what I want to do, I'm willing to pay. In spite of my wretched condition I managed to make a painting at dawn, of a peak that has fascinated me. I'll have to repeat it when I'm well, then send the best version to you.[23]

[. . .] I started a poem the day before I sickened. Here are the first four lines . . .

> "I have been one who loved the wilderness:
> Swaggered and softly crept between the mountain peaks:
> I listened long to the sea's brave music;
> I sang my songs above the shriek of desert winds."

Don't fail to write,
Love from Everett

I Shall Be Drifting South ... [24]

Letter to Bill Jacobs from Kaibab Forest, Arizona, September, 1931[25]

Dear Bill:

[. . .] One of those sunsets will always linger in my memory. It was after a day of struggle—of violent hailstorms that beat down like a thousand whiplashes, and of ferocious, relentlessly battling winds.

Then sunset, at my camp on a grassy spot in the sage. Far to the north and east the purple mesas stretched. Cloudbanks arched everywhere overhead, stretching in long lines to the horizons. There was an endless variety of cloud forms, like swirls of smoke, like puff-balls. Here and there where a sunshaft pierced a low hung cloudbar, the mesas were golden brown and vermilion.

Then the treeless western hills were rimmed with orange that faded to green and deep blue. A cold clear breeze caressed me and the full moon rolled through the clouds. The lunatic quaver of a coyote—silence and sleep.

Winter is close at hand; the maples are crimson, and flurries of yellow aspen leaves swirl about with each breeze. On many hillsides the yellow leaves have blackened, and the trees stand bare and silent. Soon the snows will be here, but I shall be drifting south toward the cactus country. [. . .]

Your Comrade,
Everett

"Cloudbanks arched everywhere overhead, . . ."

Sunset Made the Misery Worth Enduring ... [26]

Letter to Waldo, written from Grand Canyon, October 9, 1931

Dear Waldo:

[. . .] Whatever I have suffered in the months past has been nothing compared with the beauty in which I have steeped my soul. It has been a priceless experience. [. . .]

One day, as soon as we were out of town, proceeding slowly on the cowpath beside the long row of poplars, a cloudburst came. The hail beat down like a thousand whiplashes. Two small boys on a horse were thrown off into the mud when the horse saw Perry.[27] [. . .] With the wind and the sun, everything was soon dry again. We crossed the line into Arizona. Curly danced and pranced about, with shreds of bark [. . .].

The wind blew furiously and relentlessly. I was soon weary with fighting against it. It was like walking in sand. At last we left the beaten path, turning south toward the Kaibab. [. . .]

Sunset made all the misery worth enduring. Far to the north and east stretched the purple mesas, with cloudbanks everywhere above them. Some were golden brown and vermilion where sunshafts pierced the low clouds. A rainbow glowed for a moment in the south. That was a promise.

Clouds of all kinds and shapes arched overhead, stretching in long lines to the horizons. Some were like swirls of smoke. Then twilight—a rim of orange on the treeless western hills. The full moon appeared, rolling through the clouds. [. . .]

At Ribbon Falls I had more meat than Curly could eat, and offered some to Pericles. He ate three large tough pieces and wanted more, and once my companions roared at the very suggestion of a burro eating meat![28] He always likes greasy paper, cheese paper or any kind of paper. [. . .]

Your brother,
Everett

Battlements of the Colorado

I Am Not a Haggler...[29]

Letter to his mother from Superior, Arizona, October 31, 1931[30]

Dear Mother:

This evening I am starting for the Apache trail with two new burros. [. . .]

I am glad you like the pictures so well. However, remember that in my estimation, more than half of them are failures. I didn't burn them, because they had ideas which I may develop later. Do you recall the painting of a rocky butte in Monument valley, with a pale green foreground and a spotted sky? The spots were caused by frost coming from the water in the watercolor. Five of the pictures are first attempts which I later repeated with much greater success. How did you like the cliff dweller's necklace and arrowhead?

I have now another trophy to put on the wall of my imaginary studio. It is the skin of a Gila monster which I caught. It took me all morning to separate the skin from the monster, and then it wrinkled when I stretched it. It should be sewn with fine thread on a piece of felt.

For the past two days I have been in the Mexican part of Superior, which is a mining town. The Mexicans use burros to haul wood, and there are dozens of them here. I could not buy two burros with my ten dollars, so I wired you to send some money. It came this noon, and I felt much better. This is the first time on this trip that I've asked you outright for money, and needed it. Good equipment is much harder to find than food, and it is very important to get a good start. Neither Pegasus nor Perry were good burros, they were too old, and suffered under their loads. I had to travel light and carry part of the pack myself.

I am not a haggler—it is not my nature. If I knew Mexican and stayed here a week, I might be able to buy burros for what they are worth, but I don't and I can't. I bought two burros for $11.50,—$8.00 and $3.50,—pack saddle included. But when I started off today, the smaller fell down under his pack. I got $1.50 back and bought another burro for $7.00. That takes most of my money, but ten dollars was the price named for each, so you see I saved five dollars. I bought films and food and had my shoes repaired and now I have 12 cents. Only one of my burros is shod,—all the shoes in town have been sold. Perhaps I can get back the dollar that is owing me. One of my burros is brownish grey with white nose, a brown streak down each shoulder, and brown bands on his legs. The other is black with a white nose and breast. I haven't named them yet—I just bought the black one an hour ago.[31]

[. . .] This is the only place I have been where there were burros to choose from and I could not let the opportunity go by. The only work in this country is cotton picking; men are wanted for that job; but imagine picking a hundred pounds of cotton for 60 cents.

I expect to spend several days in a small canyon, and I expect to find interesting subjects in the saguaro forests. Write to Mesa. [. . .]

You would enjoy watching the Mexican children playing with baby burros.

I came from Grand Canyon to Mesa with two tourists, a man six and a half feet tall and his wife. We went through Wickenburg but I could not stop to hunt up Vernon.

Love from Everett

Idyllic Days Watching the Clouds Go By ... [32]

This first draft of a letter written from Los Angeles to ranch friends at Christmas 1931 was found among Everett's papers. His parents would be happy to hear from those who received this letter, who as yet are unknown to them.

"My little dog Curly, Cynthia, Percival, and I."

Dear friends:

Those were great days at the Veit ranch—idyllic days.[33] There I seemed to feel the true spirit of delight, the exaltation, the sense of being more than man, lying in the long cool grass, or on a flat-topped rock, looking up at the exquisitely curved, cleanly-smooth aspen limbs, watching the slow clouds go by. I would close my eyes and feel a coolness on my cheeks as the sun was covered, and then later the warmth of the sun on my eyelids. And always there was the soft rustling of aspen leaves, and a queer sense of remoteness, of feeling more beauty than I could ever portray or tell of. Have you ever felt that way?

Here is a picture of my caravan: My little dog Curly, Cynthia, Percival, and I.[34] We have traveled far over mountains and deserts, through forests and canyons, seeing strange and beautiful things, having grim and glorious experiences, but none that would make me forget your hospitality and generosity in my time of need.

Best wishes for a happy Noel.[35]
Everett

Spirit of the Wilderness Trail...[36]

This note to Bill Jacobs accompanied a burro's shoe mailed as a Christmas remembrance in 1931.

> *From my desert nightingale to you*
> *Comes this well-worn burro shoe.*

It protected his feet while he slid down rocky slopes of wild, cactus-covered hills.

It caked with snow as he descended mountain trails between white-mantled pines.

It scraped water-worn boulders as he gingerly felt his way through muddy
  mountain torrents.

Following its imprint in the red soil I tracked him many weary miles till at last old
  longears stood before me, discovered.

Sometimes in nimble haste I dodged it.

I heard it crunch pebbles in a river bed and later heard it over concrete bridges.

Heedless of Percival's dignity, a whiskered Mexican threw him down and nailed it
  to his hoof.

An Apache jerked it off.

So hang it over the door of your room, and look long at it, for it is the spirit of the
  wilderness trail.

Love from Everett

Everett's burros, descending "mountain trails between white-mantled pines."

Letters • 1932

The Willow Trees Bend Low ...[37]

Letter to his parents, written from Roosevelt Dam, April 20, 1932

Dear Father and Mother:

As I write I am sitting on the Roosevelt dam, half way up the lower side. Wild winds are shrieking in the wires, swirling in the dust heaps, and swishing the bushes. Clouds are scudding by, and the water from the power house is roaring out like a maelstrom, whipping itself to froth before it flows to Apache lake. The turbines are humming. Now the gale grows fiercer. The lake is flecked with white caps and the willow trees bend low.

Tomorrow I am going to Globe to buy provisions and I may have my shoes repaired. In a few days I shall be sending all the books except "The Brothers Karamazov." I enjoyed "Candide." The "Satyricon" was interesting, but seemed unimportant. Balzac and Dunsany were good. I think you might send "The Dance of Life." Clark has not read it, and I may reread it. I want to read either "42nd Parallel" or "Manhattan Transfer" of John Dos Passos. Also I'd like to read "Fortitude" by Walpole, and "The Magic Mountain." I still want the Anthology of Modern Poetry. [. . .]

I haven't done much painting, just a few sketches, but I've been trying to take good photographs.

Luck to everyone,
Everett

Note: Everett said that "The Dance of Life," by Havelock Ellis, was the book that had most influenced him.

"The water . . . is roaring out like a maelstrom whipping itself to froth . . ."

The Lone Trail Is Best for Me...[38]

Letter written to a friend in 1932

Dear Friend:

Three or four years ago I came to the conclusion that for me, at least, the lone trail was the best, and the years that followed strengthened my belief.

It is not that I am unable to enjoy companionship or unable to adapt myself to other people. But I dislike to bring into play the aggressiveness of spirit which is necessary with an assertive companion, and I have found it easier and more adventurous to face situations alone. There is a splendid freedom in solitude, and after all, it is for solitude that I go to the mountains and deserts, not for companionship. In solitude I can bare my soul to the mountains unabashed. I can work or think, act or recline at my whim, and nothing stands between me and the wild.[39]

Then, on occasion, I am grateful for what unusual and fine personalities I may encounter by chance, but I have learned not to look too avidly for them. I delve into myself, into abstractions and ideas, trying to arrange the other things harmoniously, but after that, taking them as they come.

As ever,
Everett

Tragedy in the Canyon of Death...[40]

Following is a quotation from Everett's diary written in the summer of 1932[41]

[. . .] I decided to call Whitey "Nuflo" after the mischievous old guardian of Rima in [W. H.] Hudson's "Green Mansions." The bay I named Jonathan because he [is] so sweet-tempered, meek, and gentle.

I fed the horses plenty of oats, then started up the side canyon under the high-perched cliff dwelling where I found the Indian necklace last year. I found the up trail steep and rough, and started, as I thought, to leave Canyon del Muerto. It was so steep I led Nuflo, and Jonathan had to be urged. Finally he fell or lay down at a rough spot about half way up. [. . .] He would not rise, so I unpacked him there. [. . .] Everything was topsy turvy. When I pulled out the pack saddle, Jonathan slid off the trail, turned over three times on the downslope, and tottered to his feet. I led him up, put Nuflo's saddle on him, packed Nuflo, and slowly descended. I did not mount Jonathan, but tied Nuflo's lead rope to the saddle horn, and we went on [. . .]. After we had gone a mile past the hogan, upstream, he began to pull back. I halted several times to see if anything was wrong. In a couple more slow miles we came to my previous campsite and stopped under a cottonwood.

I unloaded and led the horses to the bank where the grass was very sparse. I didn't hobble Jonathan. He went around in circles and didn't eat. I washed a cut on his leg and he stood still for a while, then staggered sidewise and fell into a clump of cactus.

He got groggily to his feet, tottered again and collapsed. Then I prepared myself for the worst and began looking at my map to see how near a railroad was. [. . .]

Jonathan was dead [. . .] So for me Canyon del Muerto is indeed the canyon of death—the end of the trail for gentle old Jonathan.

Canyon del Muerto

I've decided to cache my saddle in a cliff dwelling—perhaps the one where I left the cradle-board[42] last year. Now I am afoot once more and old Nuflo is my beast of burden. Black clouds are above [. . .].

I saddled Nuflo and galloped for the last time in my saddle. I led him half way up the steep slope, then shouldered the saddle and climbed. I was utterly exhausted and dripping with sweat when I reached the dwelling. I found the cradle-board, spread my old blankets on the floor of a small storehouse and laid the cradle and the saddle over them. Two of the blankets are from Grand Canyon—many a mule has had them on his back. [. . .] There was the quilt from Spurlocks, and a blanket made of a dozen gunny sacks from Superior. I wrote a note, put it under the saddle and started down the slope.

By the time I reached Nuflo it was raining violently. I was wet to the skin when we reached camp. I stood there for awhile, looking at the muddy torrent, the cascades on the cliffs, and the still form of Jonathan. The skies seemed about to open wider, so I donned my poncho, loaded Nuflo, and splashed upstream. The cloudburst drenched us, but we plodded [resolutely] forward, and soon I was in unknown country. The rain stopped. We crossed the river a thousand times. The canyon changed from red to pink, to grey, to yellow. Several times we had slippery scrambles over rocks that blocked the way, and there was some quicksand. Pines and firs were on the canyon floor, and there was one clump of aspens. At last the canyon walls were lower, but we did not find a way out. Finally I saw sheep tracks, the print of bare feet, and when I found a dry cave, I stopped, for we were both weary.

There was good grass for Nuflo. I climbed out and saw a range of purple mountains and buttes—doubtless the Lukachukais. An Indian was whistling a herd of sheep. I found a trail leading out of the canyon and returned to camp. It was late. The skies were murky, and I had not eaten since morning, so I fried some mutton and sweet bread. Then I read Browning and pondered.

How strange is reality! In the morning I shall not ride. I'll not buy another horse[43]— I haven't the money and one will do. Having only Nuflo, I'll care for him more solicitously. He'll have more oats, there'll be no more rope hobbles. I put the saddle cinch on the pack saddle and left the other in the cliff dwelling.

If I had not attempted the steep hill, Jonathan might yet be serving me but he behaved strangely the last few days. [. . .]

I sang tragic songs, looked into the coals of my campfire, listened to the song of the crickets, the murmur of the water, the clatter of Nuflo's bell (yo asoyu) and the sound of the grass being munched.

Somehow Jonathan's death has not disheartened me. I feel better for accepting the challenge to proceed without him. His death was certainly dramatic. I shall never forget how he ran sidewise, as if groping for something to lean on, found nothing, crashed to earth, and rolled over.

I doubt that anyone will ever find the saddle.[44] The baby-board was where I left it last May, except that the hoops had fallen into the bin. My printing on the board— Everett Rulan*,[45] etc—was almost obscured. The rain has washed away my tracks. The saddle is well cached. The ghosts of the cliff dwellers will guard it. I think I will not return for it, however.[46]** The clouds have gone. Stars gleam though the fir tops. It might be Christmas.

*—Everett took a boyish delight in the use of "pen" names.
**—As far as is known the saddle is still where Everett left it.

Exploring the Indian Ruins . . . [47]

Letter to his family, written from Mesa Verde, Colorado, August 25, 1932

Dear Family:

This afternoon I returned from a four-day trip to Wild Horse mesa and the North Escarpment. I visited several small cliff dwellings, some of them so situated as to be nearly inaccessible. However, I had no accidents. There was one small dwelling which could only be reached by a ledge, from six inches to a foot and a half wide. Below was a sheer drop of 50 feet or so. I had little trouble entering it, being right handed, but when it came to returning, matters were more complicated. I could not get by the narrow part with my back to the cliff, and if I faced the cliff, I had to go backwards and could not see where to set my foot. After three false starts, I finally reached level sandstone, by crawling on my knees. There was another dwelling near Horse springs, which could only be reached by working up a nearly vertical crevice, part of the way hanging by my hands. Even after that I had to cross a wide crack and crawl under a boulder on the brink. There was a little storehouse right on the face of the cliff, which I did not enter. I found a bone awl in one house.

Usually the Mesa Verde canyons are bone dry, but it has rained heavily for several days, and there was running water in places, and plenty of pot holes on the flat rocks.

There was a waterhole with cattails in it above one ruin.

I picked my way up to the mesa top and followed a grassy swale to the north brink of Mesa Verde, 8300 feet high. The sun was just setting behind a smoky cloud, casting a lurid glow over the olive drab terrain. Small lakes and canals gleamed up at the cloudless sky overhead. The lights of Cortez flickered in the distance. Soon a west wind sprang up, blowing a veil of fleecy clouds across the stars.

This morning I headed around several canyons and followed a trail southward on Wetherill mesa till I reached Rock springs. After a good rest I crossed Song canyon to Long mesa, followed the narrow ridge, peering down on some ruined towers, then into Wickiup canyon, with Buzzard's roost, a picturesque dwelling, in a cave on the opposite side. Wickiup led into Navajo canyon. Then I turned north, up Spruce canyon, up a steep trail past Spruce tree dwelling, to park headquarters, just before the postoffice closed. [. . .]

I had a good shower in the ranger quarters, and a good meal in the government mess hall. [. . .] Tomorrow I'm going to take the trips to Square Tower house, Balcony house, and Cliff palace again, scanning the horizon for California-bound motorists. Balcony house is an extremely interesting cliff dwelling, splendidly situated.

Love from Everett

Square Tower House, Mesa Verde, Colorado
Everett usually made his blockprints by referring to photographs that he had taken.

I Go to Make My Destiny ...[48]

Written by Everett Ruess during his year at the University of California, Los Angeles, in 1932[49]

One night, long ago, while I tossed restlessly upon my bed, an idea crystallized within me. In the cool night breeze I lay suddenly still, taut, and filled with a tremendous superabundance of energy that demanded outlet. My brain was busied with tense imaginings of adventure in far places.

In my mind I conjured up a thousand forgotten cities, left behind by the years; sheer grey mountains; mile upon mile of bare, unfriendly desert; cold lakes unrippled by any breeze, with depths unfathomable; jungles filled with deadly snakes, immense butterflies, brilliant colors, fever, and death. I swam in the blue seas, and in coral-tinted waters. Through insufferable heat and incessant flooding downpours I plodded forward.

On bleak, windswept coasts bordering the Antarctic, and on the broad, endless pampas of the Argentine, I pitched my camps. On the banks of the sluggish Amazon I built my fires, which glowed like earthly stars, gleaming far across the turbid waters at night. I tramped alone through wildernesses, with my food supply dwindling, and hostile forces of nature combining against me. I felt the ominous rumble and swift shock of volcanoes bursting out. The ground trembled beneath my feet as earthquakes made red ruin. On storm-lashed islands I stood, surveying far-off mountain peaks. Then I camped beneath them in shadowed valleys, watching at sunset the last bands of light that gleamed on the highest mountain tops and wherever I journeyed strange people of a foreign tongue stared at me curiously.

These are the things I saw and the experiences I lived through that night long past. Now it is night again—the night before I go. Once more I think of that which lies ahead.

Bitter pain is in store for me, but I shall bear it. Beauty beyond all power to convey shall be mine; I will search diligently for it. Death may await me; with vitality, impetuosity and confidence I will combat it. Not through cynicism and ennui will I be easy prey. And regardless of all that may befall, let me not be found to lack an understanding of the inscrutable humor of it all.

It may be that I shall turn homeward, whipped and broken; something within me tells me that it will not be so.

Cuernavaca, Rio, Titicaca, Patagonia, Quetzalcoatl, Cotopaxi—they lure me, and I shall answer their call and the call of the winding trail. Adventure is for the adventurous. My face is set. I go to make my destiny. May many another youth be by me inspired to leave the smug safety of his rut and follow fortune to other lands.

My heart beats high, but my eyelids droop; tomorrow I will go. Adventure is for the adventurous. Life is a dream. I am young, and a fool; forgive me, and read on.

Wilderness Journeys of 1932...[50]

Letter to his friends, Mr. and Mrs. Ben Reynolds, Christmas, 1932

Dear Mr. and Mrs. Ben Reynolds:

After leaving Roosevelt[51] in May, I had a very adventurous summer. Although I did not accomplish much in a tangible way, I had some worth-while experiences. There was very little routine for me. After the Henderson cowboy brothers caught my bronco, I traded him for Pacer, a middle-aged outlaw horse who knew all kinds of tricks. I forded the Salt river and climbed up the opposite side of the valley in the terrific heat. After a strenuous day I reached a cool, dark canyon below the asbestos mine, and made camp by moonlight. The next day I rode to the mountain top and stood in the wind, looking down on the lakes and blue peaks and ranges, on the sweltering valley that I had come from. I was very grateful for the pines and firs and flowers. Pacer wanted to eat all of the lupines he saw.

That night Pacer broke his rope and started home. I tracked him until it was dark, and I saw him on the road ahead. Then began a furious chase. He was hobbled, but he galloped nevertheless. Past black canyons, blue vistas, forests and fields we raced in the moonlight. Whenever I was just about to catch him, he would break into a gallop again, and I couldn't seem to get around him. Finally he tired and I caught him and rode bareback to the darkened camp, arriving late at night.

Then I went up and over the mountain, coming down a steep trail to Cherry creek and Flying H ranch. I killed two rattlesnakes which were coiled in the trail. After a day or two at the ranch I went up the creek and explored some side canyons with unusual cliff dwellings. There is one dwelling three stories high in a narrow crack in the cliff which goes back about a hundred feet, then turns and comes out in a balcony on the other side of the cliff. I had to find my own way up the canyon. No one had been there in a long time, and the trails disappeared every now and then. I followed along the creek, crossing and recrossing, until I came to waterfalls Pacer couldn't climb. Then we forced our way through the dense manzanita brush until we were on the plateau. Four or five times Pacer tried to get away from me in pastures. He was not in condition either, so in Pleasant valley I traded him for two little burros, Peggy and Wendy. We crossed the Mogollons, stopping at ranches now and then. The people in the cow country were all very friendly and hospitable.

Peggy and Wendy were fine little burros, friendly and good, always staying with each other, very droll and lovable in their actions. I used always to carry corn for them. I myself made many meals on parched corn and jerky. Before long, however, it became evident that Peggy was going to be a mother. When I was on my way to Holbrook from Zeniff, a rancher stopped his car and invited me to stay at his ranch as long as I pleased. It was hailing at the time, so I turned back to his place, where I stayed for a whole month. I learned to brand cows and wrangle horses. I did not learn to milk, and I was thrown from a horse once. I did all kinds of work, and at the end of the month my rancher gave me a saddle, another rancher gave me a horse, and I bought another old horse for six dollars. (Note: See pages 19–21 for more about Everett's two horses.)

Camp in Deserted Hogan

Northward I rode, wandering through the Painted desert and the Navajo country. I spent days serene and tempestuous in Canyon de Chelly, then traveled up Canyon del Muerto in the shade of sheer, incurving cliffs, breathtakingly chiseled and gloriously colored. I passed the last Navajo encampments and stopped for a space in a deserted hogan, constructed of smooth clean-limbed cottonwood, with singing water at the door and sighing leaves overhead—tall, gracefully arched trees screening the sky with a glistening pattern of dappled green, and above and beyond the gorgeous vermilion cliffs. All day I would brood in the cool of the hogan, lying on the diamond saddle blanket I bought from old Dilatsi. Beneath it was a swirl of crisp brown leaves, over the earth floor. Now and then a trickle of sand pouring through a crack in the roof would sift down, rustling the leaves, and the circle of sunshine from the skylight would move from hour to hour. At evening I would go out into the glade and climb high above the river to the base of the cliff. I would gather scarlet flowers and come down when the stars gleamed softly. Sighing winds would eddy down the canyon, swaying the tree tops. Then the leaves would cease to tremble; only the sound of rippling water would continue, and the spirit of peace and somnolence would pervade the grove, as the red embers of my fire one by one turned black, and shadows deepened into a gently surging slumber.

Everett, Nuflo (left), and Jonathan, pausing in Canyon de Chelly, Arizona, 1932.

It was while I was staying at this hogan that I made the drawing for the print which I am sending you.

When I was climbing out of the canyon, Jonathan, my gentle old pack-horse, missed his footing on a steep trail, and was killed. I cached the saddle in an unvisited cliff dwelling and went on afoot, leading tricky old Nuflo, my white horse. When I reached the Lukachukais of New Mexico, I could go no further, so I rested at the edge of a lake among the aspens and pines. I saw a big brown bear. Then I went on toward Mesa Verde, but before I was halfway to Shiprock my strength failed me, and I stopped again in the heart of the lonely desert, staying in an ancient high-vaulted hogan, with juniper logs night-black, darkened by smoke of many fires.

White Horse Falls in River

In the Mancos river, Nuflo fell into the flooded stream from a narrow trail on a ledge, and I had to jump in after him to save the pack. The camera was spoiled by the alkali water, and I could hardly get the tarpaulin out. Nuflo was not hurt, but it began to rain as soon as I spread things out to dry.

I went through the Ute reservation and entered Mesa Verde from the canyons. There I spent the month of August. Part of the time I stayed in the ranger quarters. I explored the mesa and had some adventures in Wild Horse canyon. Then I turned Nuflo loose with a band of other horses. In late August I decided I would like to go to college for awhile, so I started west, but I stopped for several days at the Grand Canyon, descending alone to the depths, to submerge myself in the steep silence, to be overcome by the fearful immensity, and to drown everything in the deafening roar of the Colorado, watching its snaky writhings and fire-tongued leapings until I was entranced.

In the canyon I killed my eighth rattler of the summer—a rare species found only in the Grand Canyon.

But I turned my back on the solitudes, and one chill, foggy dawn, I arrived in Los Angeles, where I discarded my sombrero and boots for city garb.

I don't belong in college (U.C.L.A.) but it has been another experience, and anything that happens is of value as an experience, when it's over. Today was the last day of school this year, and I think I shall go up the Coast to Carmel and Point Lobos to do some work and consider a few problems. After months in the desert and months in the city, I long for the sea caves, the breakers crashing in the tunnels, the still tropi-colored lagoons, the jagged cliffs and ancient warrior cypresses.

Of all the families I have met, there was none I liked better than yours, and none where I felt more at home. I will always remember your hospitality toward me. It was deep-rooted and sincere, I know, and has meant very much to me.

I wish you a very happy Christmas and a blithesome New Year.

Sincerely,
Everett

Letters and Poems • 1933

I Am Going to Shoulder My Pack...[52]

Letter to Fritz Loeffler written at Los Angeles, May 23, 1933[53]

Dear Fritz:

[. . .] When I left Mesa Verde, as you probably know, I got a ride to Gallup with a tourist going to Grand Canyon. I had only two or three dollars then. You may remember that certain of the rangers were amused at my idea of getting a ride with all my dunnage. [. . .] Later I was fairly stranded in Needles, and was reduced to wiring for help, but the wire was never received and I got a ride straight through, arriving in a dense fog in Los Angeles in a strange part of the city.

I hadn't been home a week before I heard the call again, and went inland to Red Rock canyon for a few days. Then I followed your suggestion and enrolled at U.C.L.A., taking geology, philosophy, English history, English, gym and military drill. I'm glad I went, but I'm glad it's over. College was a valuable episode, but I didn't let it get a strangle hold on me.

During the three weeks vacation at Christmas, I went up to Carmel by the sea, did some good work, and had some splendid experiences. I rode a black horse on the cool velvet beach at the edge of the surf, splashing through the salt water at times, and galloping beside the waves.

I went back to school in January and finished the semester last month. It seems much longer. (Note: Everett received an honorable dismissal, with no conditions.)

I have been taking a self-prescribed course in human relations, and I have taken a more than usual interest in music of late. Music means more to me than any other art, I think. Have you been enjoying your violin? I have several friends with fine victrolas and recorded music, and I have some myself and can borrow more. I've been reading heavily too—philosophy, poetry, travel, psychology, etc. Also I have been writing occasionally.

[. . .] In a month or so when it is hot, I am going to shoulder my pack and go up in the Sierras, with some rice and oatmeal, a few books, paper and paints. It will be good to be on the trail again. A friend of mine is just preparing for a trip to Utah, and it is hard for me to stay. After the Sierras, I may stay in San Francisco and have the experience of another city. Perhaps later I'll go up the coast. Next year I expect to spend almost the whole year in the red wastes of the Navajo country, painting industriously.

I was certainly glad to have your letter.

Your friend,
Everett

Fragments [54]

High on a cliff enthroned, I have watched a silver stream
Threading between red walls, and faintly rose to me
The mellow sound of sheep bells, and
The weird wild chanting of an Indian shepherd. [55]

* * *

The breakers crashing in the sea-caves,
The still lagoons, the ancient warrior cypresses. [56]

Granite and Cypress

A ride on the velvet beach,
Hoof's splashing in the broad, ribbony edge of the surf. [57]

* * *

Broad peaceful lake,
Mysteriously vast at twilight;
Sacred hush,
Glimmering waters open to the sky.

—by Everett Ruess, 1933

It Is Always Time to Live... [58]

Letter to his brother Waldo from Sequoia National Park, June 8, 1933

Dear Waldo:

Thus far, I have been free of watches and clocks. I never wonder what time it is, because for myself it is always time to live. I've had a number of new experiences not all intense, but nevertheless enjoyable. I've been meeting people and climbing trails. I was in a snowstorm on a mountain top a few days ago. Life is pleasant, but things will not finally resolve themselves till I hit the trail for Kern canyon in a week or so. At the present, the high country is choked with snow. I traded a print for some credit in the store here, and have a possible buyer for a painting I made on Sunset rock. I've met several boys from the reforestation camps.[59] They are not a bad lot, but I couldn't bear to be tied down. What I miss most here is intellectual companionship, but that is always difficult to find, and I have met a few interesting individuals.

Don't leave your problems to be solved by Time—the solution might be adverse.

Your brother,
Everett

Note: The mountains of the desert Southwest and the mountains of the high Sierra chain and all mountains have a kinship. Contrary to the ideas of many city-folk, the deserts of the Southwest rise into numerous mountains and forests, with cool lakes. So on a few pages here are included high Sierra letters by Everett, pages 28–32 . "An Early Start" was taken at sunrise in the high Sierra, but might as well have been made in Kaibab forest. Everett's diary of 1933 in Sequoia and Yosemite parks and the high Sierra, perhaps his best writing, may later be published, with appropriate illustrations.

I Have Lived Intensely ... [60]

To friends from the high Sierra in 1933

Dear Friends:

During the last few weeks, I have been having the time of my life. Much of the time I feel so exuberant that I can hardly contain myself. The colors are so glorious, the forests so magnificent, the mountains so splendid, and the streams so utterly, wildly, tumultuously, effervescently joyful that to me at least, the world is a riot of intense sensuous delight. In addition to all, the people are genial and generous and happy, and everyone seems to be at his best.

Late last night I walked the four miles up the road. With a pack of groceries on my back, I swung irresistibly up the starlit road between the pillared sequoias. I drank at a rushing mountain stream, and strode gallantly up, singing some Dvorak melodies till the forest boomed with my rollicking song. Then the transmuted melody of Beethoven, Brahms, and the Bolero rang through the listening forest. I rocked from side to side of the road. I spun around in circles, looking up at the stars, and swung exultantly down the white pathway to adventure. Adventure is for the adventurous.

Oh, I have lived intensely, drinking deep! One day I rode 35 miles over mountain trails with cowboy comrades. We forded the swollen rivers, putting our feet on the saddle, plunging through the foamy, buffeting snow-water, rolling like ships in a heavy sea. We galloped up cliff-sides and found our way over unknown trails in the starlight. While my horse groped his way up the darkened mountainside far above the rushing stream, I leaned back in my saddle looking at the towering ranges, the looming ridge above, the intensely brilliant stars, and the waning moon. We delivered a horse to an outrider at a battered old cabin on the skyline, then in the dim starlight, in the hours before dawn, we came down the mountain. We loped for miles, swerving and wheeling at full speed on a winding river-road, following its pale gleam through tunnels of foliage.

Then I was in a snowstorm on the mountain top, helping a ranger from Alaska probe for and recover signs broken and buried in the snow. We sat on our feet and slid down the snow slopes, speeding uncontrollably past mountain lakes, thickets of writhen, snakelike, contorted aspens, and cherry and willow with bark of coppery sheen.

I swam in a deep pool below one waterfall and above another. The granite sides were so slippery that I could hardly draw myself out when I had frolicked enough.

With great enjoyment I read of the unrestrained exploits of Gargantua, Granzousier, Picrochole, and the monk. The other night I ate a Gargantuan mess of sandwiches and fried yams while I read about Pantagruel and Panurge, how they discomfited Impgarva and his giants. When the fire faded, the embers took on a more intense glow, the trees loomed higher, and the starlight poured straight down.

So now you know how I disport myself. Do you, in your turn, inform me of your adventures. I hope you two also are on the crest of the wave, or at least not in its trough. [. . .]

Irrepressibly,
Everett

Over Unknown Canyon Trails by Moonlight ...[61]

To Lawrence Janssens from the Sierras in June, 1933[62]

Dear Lawrence:

Right now I am sitting on a hill overlooking the Marble fork of the Kaweah river. The colors are glorious—fleecy white clouds, a clear blue sky, distant blue hills flecked with snow, tall pines all around me, monstrous grey glacial boulders and patches of sunlit moss on the fir trees. The snow-water rushes and pounds through its rocky channel, tumbling frothily into lucent green pools.

Here I seem to be in my element. Save for the lack of intellectual companionship, which is not utter, and is troublesome wherever I am, and for a few trifling disturbances, I have nothing to lament. More than ever before, I have succeeded in stopping the clock. I need no timepiece, knowing that now is the time to live.

I have lived intensely on several occasions here. Down in Three Rivers, below in the cow country, I rode 35 miles in one day, fording a river so swollen with snows that I had to put my feet on the saddle horn. I rode my horse up cliff banks, over unknown canyon trails by moonlight, watched the stars as we groped over the darkened path, and climbed to a lonesome cabin on skyline. Later I loped for miles on a winding river road, following its pale gleam under tunnels of foliage.

Again I climbed the mountain pass, fought a snowstorm, and scraped through three feet of snow to recover broken trail signs. Then I set my feet and slithered down long snowy aisles, swerving and careening past groves of writhen, snakelike, tortured aspens, and past willow trees with bark of coppery sheen, incense cedar, red fir, and white fir.

Your friend,
Everett

I Had a Delightful Trip to Siberian Pass ...

To Ned Frisius from Tokopah Valley in August, 1933[63]

Dear Ned:

[. . .] After we parted, I had a delightful trip to Siberian pass and down Golden trout creek. I took up the sport of fishing, practising it with necessary two-day intervals. A black gnat, six feet of line, and a willow pole were all my equipment, and I caught several limits of fish. Betsy, Grandma, and I crossed the rickety bridge on the Kern, which swayed up, down and sidewise. Later I stopped for lunch in Rattlesnake canyon, but as I was looking for firewood, I found a willow pole, and the rest of the day was given over to piscatorial delights. I reached Mineral King on Sunday morning. That night in Cliff creek I caught my biggest stream fish. I could not close my fist on him!

For the last week or more, I have had blood poisoning in my right hand, but I can bend two fingers now, and I hope to start north in four or five days. I am typing this with my left hand. [. . .]

> Sincerely your friend,
> Everett

Everett and friends, getting "an early start."

All Is a Golden Dream ...[64]

To a friend in Visalia from Kaweah canyon in 1933[65]

Dear Friend:

I have been feeling so happy and filled to overflowing with the beauty of life that I felt I must tell you. All is a golden dream, with mysterious, high-rushing winds leaning down to caress me, and warm and perfect colors flowing before my eyes. Time and the need of time have ceased entirely. A gentle, dreamy haze fills my soul, the unreal rustling of the aspens stirs my senses and the surpassing beauty and perfection of everything fills me with quiet joy, and a deep overflowing love for my world.

My solitude is unbroken. Above, the white, castellated cliffs glitter fairylike against the turquoise sky. The wild silences have enfolded me, unresisting.

Beauty and peace have been with me wherever I have gone. At night I have watched pale granite towers in the dim starlight, aspiring to the powdered sky, tremulous and fantastic in the melting darkness. I have watched white-maned rapids, shaking their crusts in wild abandon, surging, roaring, overwhelming the senses with their white fury, only to froth and foam down the current into lucent green pools, quiet and clear in the mellow sunlight.

On the trail the musical tinkle of the burro bells mingles with the sound of wind and water, and is heard only subconsciously.

On the lakes at night the crescent moon gleams liquidly in the dark water, mists drift and rise like lifting enchantments, and tall, shadowed peaks stand guard in watchful silence.

Aloof and in the midst of beauty I wish to share with you these living dreams. The tall pines lift proudly to the starry sky. The river rushes singing down the canyon. I too am singing in my heart, and I sing the song of the wilderness.[66]

Yours,
Everett

Everett's Quiz from the Desert [67]

(To his father)[68]

1. Is life only sensation?
2. Is service the true end of life?
3. Can a strong mind maintain independence and strength if it is not rooted in material independence?
4. Are not all people dependent upon one another?
5. Do all things follow the attainment of Truth?
6. Is bodily love empty or to be forgotten?
7. Can one ask too much of life?
8. Does life have infinite potentialities?
9. Must pain spring from pleasure?
10. Are pain and pleasure equally desirable and necessary?
11. Is the goal of life thought and love, untouched by the material?
12. Is pleasure right for all, but selfish for one?
13. Can one be happy while others are miserable?
14. Can one be fine without great sacrifice?
15. Can one make great sacrifices without submerging oneself?
16. Should one submerge oneself in sacrifice?
17. Does not one serve most by doing what one does best?
18. Is it possible to be truly unselfish?
19. How is it possible for everyone to give more than he is given?
20. Can one give by receiving?
21. Is there any fulfillment that endures as such, besides death?
22. Is there anything perpetual besides change?
23. Is passage from the sensual to the intellectual to the spiritual a correct progression of growth, and if so should the growth be hastened?

Wilderness Song [69]

I have been one who loved the wilderness;
Swaggered and softly crept between the mountain peaks;
I listened long to the sea's brave music;
I sang my songs above the shriek of desert winds.

On canyon trails when warm night winds were blowing,
Blowing, and sighing gently through the star-tipped pines,
Musing, I walked behind my placid burro,
While water rushed and broke on pointed rocks below.

I have known a green sea's heaving; I have loved
Red rocks and twisted trees and cloudless turquoise skies,
Slow sunny clouds, and red sand blowing;
I have felt the rain and slept behind the waterfall.

In cool sweet grasses I have lain[70] and heard
The ghostly murmur of regretful winds
In aspen glades, where rustling silver leaves
Whisper wild sorrows to the green-gold solitudes.

I have watched the shadowed clouds pile high;
Singing I rode to meet the splendid, shouting storm
And fought its fury till the hidden sun
Foundered in darkness, and the lightning heard my song.

Say that I starved; that I was lost and weary;
That I was burned and blinded by the desert sun;
Footsore, thirsty, sick with strange diseases;
Lonely and wet and cold . . . but that I kept my dream!

Always I shall be one who loves the wilderness;
Swaggers and softly creeps between the mountain peaks;
I shall listen long to the sea's brave music;
I shall sing my song above the shriek of desert winds.

—published in the *Los Angeles Daily News*, May 10, 1935

Letters and Poems • 1934

I Do Not Regret My Freedom...[71]

To his father, Christopher G. Ruess, from San Francisco, January 2, 1934

[. . .] I have three million-dollar endowments [. . .] that I am sure of, and I don't have to go begging. I have my very deep sensitivities to beauty, to music, and to nature. In addition, thanks to you and to mother, I have an intellect that is capable of analysis and of grappling with things almost anywhere I turn. [. . .] I [. . .] do not regret my freedom. On all sides I meet people who are not able to follow things up as I am doing, and it is not I who envy them. [. . .]

Mountain Shadows

What I Most Wanted to Do...[72]

To his father, Christopher G. Ruess, from San Francisco, January 27, 1934

[. . .] What you say is partly true, in your remark that I have done what I most wanted to do in spite of the world. Today I found three letters from friends in various quarters of whom it is by no means true. They have been wallowing in the shallows of life this past year—not growing nor having new and enlarging experiences, driven partly or wholly by circumstances into lives that they themselves consider ignoble, stale, and depressing. [. . .]

I Had a Strange Ride Last Night...[73]

To his parents from Lukachukai mountains, Arizona, May, 1934

Dear Father and Mother:

I had a strange ride last night. At twilight, by the side of a rushing stream, on the edge of the desert, I packed and saddled my burros. The half moon had an orange glow as I rode on the trail up the mountains. Behind us, thunder boomed on the desert, and black clouds spread. We soon climbed above the red sandstone cliffs, and tall pines and firs stood against the night sky. Moaning winds swept down the canyon, bending the tree tops, and clouds hid the moon.

Silently old Cockleburrs, my saddle burro, carried me upward through the night, and Leopard followed noiselessly with the pack. Grotesque shapes of trees reared themselves against the darkening sky, and disappeared into blackness as the trail turned. For a while the northerly sky was clear, and stars shone brilliantly through the pine boughs. Then darkness closed upon us, only to be rent by lurid flashes of lightning and thunder that seemed to shake the earth. The wind blew no longer, and we traveled in an ominous murky calm, occasionally shattered by more lightning and thunder. Finally the clouds broke and rain spattered down as I put on my slicker. We halted under a tall pine. The burros stood motionless with head down and water dripped off their ears.

In half an hour the rain stopped, and the skies cleared. By moonlight we climbed to the rim of the mountain, and I looked over vast stretches of desert. Thirty miles away was the dim hulk of Shiprock, a ghostly galleon in a sea of sand.

We turned northward on the nearby level top of the mountain and winding through the glades of aspen we came to three peaceful lakes, gleaming silver in the moonlight. Under a clump of low sprawling oaks we stopped, and there I unpacked, turning the burros out to graze on the tall meadow grass.

Now it is afternoon. Flowers nod in the breeze, and wild geese are honking on the lake. I have just been for a long leisurely ride on Leopard, skirting the edge of the mountain, riding through thickets of rustling aspen, past dark, mysterious lakes, quiet and lonely in the afternoon silence. Two friendly horses were belly deep in a pond, swishing their tails and placidly chewing rushes and swamp grass. Four other horses, cream and black, sorrel, buckskin and grey, made a splendid picture as they loped off on the edge of a valley, under towering pine trees. No human being disturbed the brooding silence of the mountain.

> "For let the mad wild birds of dawn be calling me,
> I will abide in this forest of pines."

That is something I remember from "Green Symphony," John Gould Fletcher's vivid poem of forests. Have you read it? Kayenta is my next address.

Love from Everett

Shiprock, Navajo Reservation, New Mexico, rising like "a ghostly galleon in a sea of sand."

I Had to Make a Painting ...[74]

To Mrs. Emily Ormond from near Kayenta, Arizona, May 2, 1934

Dear Mrs. Ormond:

Viljalmar Stefansson, the Arctic explorer, says that adventures are a sign of unpreparedness and incompetence. I think he is largely right, nevertheless I like adventure and enjoy taking chances when skill and fortitude play a part. If we never had any adventures, we would never know what stuff was in us.

So last night I had quite a satisfactory adventure. [. . .]

Then I rode on again, and for a while I was very blithe, singing lustily into the wind, and remembering some magnificent music. Then the sky grew inky and I urged the burros onward, shouting, "Sintlo, Kelly, dill yago!" We passed right under the towering bulk of Agathla, popularly called El Capitan, and I had to make a painting. It is a splendid rock, with spires and pinnacles of black volcanic stone. I did not trouble to finish the sketch, but even so it was almost dark, and it was five or six miles to a campsite.

So I soon dismounted and drove both burros, shouting until they fairly loped. [. . .]

Though not all my days are as wild as this, each one holds its surprises, and I have seen almost more beauty than I can bear. Many times, in the search for waterholes and cliff dwellings, I trusted my life to crumbling sandstone and angles little short of the perpendicular, startling myself when I came out whole and on top.

So tell Mable what kind of burros I have; they are grazing peacefully now, like good little donkeys, and haven't strayed all day.

Cordially,
Everett

The Burros Bolted into the Night...

Letter to Waldo from Kayenta, Arizona, May 3, 1934

Dear Waldo:

[. . .] Today I am starting for Chin Lee, Canyon de Chelly, the Lukachukais and the Carrizos.

I had many wild adventures in the last two weeks, not the least exciting of which occurred the night before last. I had ridden fully 25 miles that day, fighting a raging gale all day. The seas of purple loco bloom were buffeted about by the wind, and the sand blew in riffles across our tracks, obscuring them almost at once.

Late in the day, we passed under the towering bulk of Agathla, with its spires and pinnacles of volcanic stone, and I had to make a painting. When I was through, it was nearly dark, and as it was five or six miles to the camping place I had in mind, I dismounted and drove the burros at a trot. Inky clouds spread across the sky, and soon it was black dark. We crossed a broad, level valley, and climbed out on the farther rim at a fast walk. The road was hardly visible. A mile beyond, just as I was about to head the burros off to the rocks to search for a hogan, they suddenly bolted into the night. I ran until my lungs were afire, and heard the pack thumping away in the distance. I kept on to the creek, and found no trace of them. I thought of the smashed saddles and broken kyaks, their contents scattered broadcast, of the crushed camera, and the paintings lying in the rain. I knew Cockleburrs (the pack donkey) could not strip the pack without smashing it. And while I went after the burros, who might be kicking their heels miles away, the Navajos would be gathering up my scattered belongings.

It was only a mile or two to Kayenta. I started to walk there to ask help of my Mormon friend, but a mile away, I turned about and went back. It was not that I couldn't stand being laughed at by the whole town, for it really was funny, and such things don't bother me. But it would be asking too much of the Mormon, and anyway, for a long time I had flattered myself that I could "take it," and always had, without complaint, so I thought this was a good time to show myself.

I searched about in the darkness and the rocks, but found no traces other than two saddle blankets which had slipped out. With these I felt my way to the hogan and soon had a fire blazing. As there was nothing to eat or drink, I watched the stars through the skyhole as they appeared and disappeared, behind the racing clouds.

I would sleep until the fire died down, then build it up and nap again. As I went forth at dawn, it began to rain. A couple of miles off, I found tracks in the hard sand. Then, almost before I knew it, I was face to face with Cockleburrs. I had builded better than I knew; his pack was still intact! He was standing stock-still, looking very foolish. Leopard was nearby, equally sheepish, his saddle under him, but unhurt. The camera and canteen were lost from it, but in half an hour's circling I found them both, little harmed.

So we three went slowly back to last night's point of departure, and as we neared the hogan, the fire blazed up and smoke curled out above. I felt perfectly delighted with everything, gave the burros an extra ration of oats, hobbled them out, and put on the pot to cook my supper and breakfast.

37

I had many other thrills when I trusted my life to crumbling sandstone and angles little short of the perpendicular, in the search for waterholes and cliff dwellings. Often I was surprised myself when I came out alive and on top. [. . .]

Your brother,
Everett

Errant burros, enjoying "an extra ration of oats."

I Shall Always be a Rover ...[75]

Letter to Bill Jacobs from Chilchinbetoh, Arizona, May 5, 1934

Dear Bill:

Once more I am roaring drunk with the lust of life and adventure and unbearable beauty. I have the devil's own conception of a perfect time; adventure seems to beset me on all quarters without my even searching for it; I find gay comradeships and lead the wild, free life wherever I am. And yet, there is always an undercurrent of restlessness and wild longing; "the wind is in my hair, there's a fire in my heels," and I shall always be a rover, I know. Always I'll be able to scorn the worlds I've known like half burnt candles when the sun is rising, and sally forth to others now unknown. I'm game; I've passed my own rigorous tests, and I know that I can "take it." And I'm lucky too, or have been. Time and again, my life or all my possessions have swung on the far side of the balance, and always thus far I've come out on top and unharmed, even toughened by the chances I've taken.

"Live blindly and upon the hour; the lord, who was the future, died full long ago." Among others, I've tried that way, and found it good too. Finality does not appall me, and I seem always to enjoy things the more intensely because of the certainty that they will not last. Oh it's a wild, gay time! Life can be rich to overflowing. I've been so happy that I can't think of containing myself. I've no complaints to make, and time and the world are my own, to do with as I please. And I've had it up and down; no tedious, humdrum middle course has been mine, but a riotously plunging and soaring existence.

Again I say, it's a wild, gay time. I've slept under hundreds of roofs, and shall know others yet. I've carved a way for myself, turned hostile strangers into staunch friends, swaggered and sung through surplus of delight where nothing and no one cared whether I lived or died.

The things I've loved and given up without a complaint have returned to me doubled. There's no one in the world I envy.

Fling a flouncing fandango to foil the fast following funereal future! Seize the burning present and follow after your own seeking and your heart's desire. Then one delight will lead to the next and deeper, as swiftly as your own nature will allow. You are your only barrier to flaming ecstasy, and gold is where you find it.

Around me stretches the illimitable desert, and far off and near by are the outposts of suffering, struggling, greedy, grumbling humanity. But I don't choose to join on that footing. I'm sorry for it and I help it when I can, but I'll not shoulder its woes. To live is to be happy; to be carefree, to be overwhelmed by the glory of it all. Not to be happy is a living death.

Alone I shoulder the sky and hurl my defiance and shout the song of the conqueror to the four winds, earth, sea, sun, moon, and stars. I live!

Everett

I Have Been Flirting with Death ... [76]

Letter to Edward Gardner from Canyon de Chelly, Arizona, in May, 1934

Dear Edward:

[. . .] For five days I have been in this canyon. I have not seen an Indian, and it is a week since I saw a whiteskin. Day before yesterday I very narrowly escaped being gored to death by a wild bull, and there was a harrowing sequel when he discovered my camp that night, somewhile between midnight and dawn. Yesterday I did some miraculous climbing on a nearly vertical cliff, and escaped unscathed from that too. One way and another, I have been flirting pretty heavily with death, the old clown.

Now the shadow of a night cliff has fallen on my camp, to remain until dawn. On the opposite canyon wall, towering sheer above, I watch the fantastic gyrating shadows of two buzzards, that wheel and slant in the upper sunlight.

Strange sad winds sweep down the canyon, roaring in the firs and the tall pines, swaying their crests. I don't know how you feel about it, Edward, but I can never accept life as a matter of course. Much as I seem to have shaped my own way, following after my own thinking and my own desires, I never cease to wonder at the impossibility that I live. Even when to my senses the world is not incredibly beautiful or fantastic, I am overwhelmed by the appalling strangeness and intricacy of the curiously tangled knot of life, and at the way that knot unwinds, making everything clear and inevitable, however unfortunate or wonderful. [. . .]

Now the last light lingers on the topmost rim of the red sandstone cliffs, touching a lone tree with gold. Now that has faded. The flowers are closing, and the cicadas sing shrilly. [. . .]

I'm enclosing for you a single gay blossom of a scarlet bugler. [. . .]

Give my well-wishes to your sister and Alec and the rest of the family. Was the final performance of the Ninth Symphony as good as the rehearsal? [. . .]

Sincerely your friend,
Everett

P.S. From up the canyon, I hear an ominous muttering and bellowing, rapidly coming nearer. Evidently Black Sir Taurus and I are going to have it out again, and I'll leave you in the suspense I'm in. But if this letter reaches you, the chances are I shall have ousted him. Now he is much closer; what ugly long horns he has, and how unbelievably horrible his furious bellowing! Meanwhile a melody of Brahms recurs to me.

I Stayed with the Navajo ... [77]

Letter to a writer friend[78] from Kayenta, Arizona, June 17, 1934

Dear X:

[. . .] Personally I have no least desire for fame. I feel only a stir of distaste when I think of being called "the well known author" or "the great artist." I fear, or rather, the rest of the world should fear, that I am becoming quite antisocial. I have no desire to bend my efforts toward entertaining the bored and blase world. And that's what writing amounts to—or at least, your kind, I think. Your stories, if polished and published, would serve to divert various morons. They would help them to occupy a few hours of their lives in reading about the imagined activities of fictitious characters. Then, more thoroughly satisfied with their own more peaceful or otherwise superior lives, they would use the magazine to start a fire or sell it to the junk man.

I hope this gets you down, for I feel like puncturing the stupid satisfaction and silly aspirations of the world this morning. And not because I am wounded either, for I am myself in fine fettle. [. . .]

A while ago I spent all my money for a bracelet and have been broke most of the while since. It is a beautiful thing; I had never thought of owning one, but it seemed to fit so well, and I liked the design and the three turquoises so well, that I have never regretted the purchase. By day it is like a bit of the sky on my wrist, when my hand is on the saddle horn, and by firelight the stones have a rich, greenish luster, as they reflect the leaping flames.

But one of my trader friends asked me as soon as he saw it, "How much did it cost?" He saw it only as merchandise.

Three evenings ago, I rode out into the open desert and the sage, with the vast reaching vermilion mesas and the distant blue mountains, glad to be alone and free.

I painted at sunset—dark towering buttes, with pure clean lines, and golden light on the western cliffs as the sun went down. Then I rode on while the new moon, a silver crescent, gleamed in the deepening blue of the night sky. A fire winked and blazed a mile or two away, at the foot of a lonely butte. As it was in my direction, I steered my course by it, thinking I might stop for a cup of coffee. The fire disappeared as we descended the little dips, but always appeared again, burning steadily. At last we reached it and I dismounted and entered the circle, making a greeting. There was an old grandmother, not thin, with straying locks of white hair, and the old man, her husband; two younger women, their babies, and a young buck.

When I asked Shimassohn, the grandmother, for some coffee, she beamed, asked me questions, gave me tea and coffee, pushed naneskade (bread) toward me, and urged me to eat. [. . .]

I have often stayed with the Navajo; I've known the best of them, and they are fine people. I have ridden with them on their horses, eaten with them, and even taken part in their ceremonies. Many are the delightful encounters, and many the exchanges of gifts I've had with them. They have many faults; most of them are not very clean, and they will steal anything from a stranger, but never if you approach them with trust as a friend. Their weird wild chanting as they ride the desert is often magnificent, with a high pitched, penetrating quality.

The people I stopped with were Utes, come down from the North. After breakfast of hot goat's milk gravy, mutton, and Dutch oven bread, I brought in my burros as the two men and the grandmother were preparing to ride to post 15 miles off. Grandmother led her horse over the hill, as the Indian women will never mount in the presence of a white man.

I rode all morning over sandy dunes of vermilion sand with broom and sunflower on the ridges and nodding grass plumes. Finally, I reached a little unnamed canyon where I had camped before and rode to the very end of it, hoping against hope that the waterhole would not be dry.

There was just enough for me and my burros. Some loose horses came in, and would have drunk it all if I had not been first. There were other holes further off which they could find.

So I unpacked under a tall, arched *pinon* tree, unfastened the diamond hitch, took off the kyaks and saddles, gave the burros some oats, curried them, and turned them out to grass in a spacious bend of the canyon. There are two cliff dwellings there, one barely accessible.

After a refreshing bath at the edge of the little dwindling pool at the foot of the cliff, I wandered in the canyon and watched the burros, then worked over my equipment. This trip has been longer than I expected, for I have been in many beautiful places, and did not wish to taste, but to drink deep. I have wandered over more than 400 miles with the burros, these last six weeks, paying no attention to trails, except as they happened to serve me, and finding my water as I went. I never went two days without discovering it.

Tomorrow I shall start for Navajo mountain and the wild country near it. At Oljeto (Moonlight water) an old timer will help me shoe my burros in preparation for the miles and miles of bare sandstone ridges that must be traversed.

Here in Kayenta I have been staying with Lee Bradley, my best friend here. He is a tall, commanding figure of a man, half white, and combining the best qualities of both races. He is influential in the tribe, and has the mail contract and several other government contracts. His wife is Indian.

41

Lee's house is a rambling adobe structure. There are several pets—a baby prairie dog, rabbits, a young goat, cats, and Kisge, who is undoubtedly the father or grandfather of my dog Curly. He is an enormous shaggy dog, with the same brown eyes and wide face.

Jose Garcia, my good friend at Chilchinbetoh, whose rare old Spanish hospitality I enjoyed last month, was killed a few weeks ago, riding the load on a truck. A wheel came off, and the whole load fell on him.

There is an archaeological expedition in town now. Some pretty likeable and intelligent young fellows are in it, and I expect to visit their camp when I come back from the mountains.

Summer draws on, the shrill song of the cicadas is over, and the scarlet cactus blooms are gone. Columbine and sego lily have vanished from the canyons. Now only the sunflower, and in damp shaded places, the scarlet bugler, are found.

. . . In the throbbing heat of desert noon, siestas are in order, and I have been traveling at dawn and sunset, and by moonlight.

Did you get "The Purple Land?" I liked your line about "the kingly insolence of desert battlements."

I shall be returning to Kayenta in a month or so, before finally leaving for El Canyon Grande, and you can reach me here. So, until then, live gaily, live deeply, and wrest from life some of its infinite possibilities.

Your friend,
Everett

When I Go I Leave No Trace... [79]

Letter to Bill Jacobs from War God Springs, Navajo Mountain, Arizona, June 19, 1934[80]

Dear Bill:

A high wind is roaring in the tops of the tall pines. The moon is just rising on the rim of the desert, far below. Stars gleam through the pine boughs, and through the filmy clouds that move across the night sky. Graceful, slim-trunked aspens reach upward through the towering pines. Their slender, curving branches are white in the firelight, and an occasional downward breeze flickers their pale green leaves.

The beauty of this place is perfect of its kind; I could ask for nothing more. A little spring trickles down under aspens and white fir. By day the marshy hollow is aswarm with gorgeous butterflies; tiger and zebra swallowtails, the anglewings, the mourning-cloak, and others. There are a hundred delightful places to sit and dream, friendly rocks to lean against, springy beds of pine needles to lie on and look up at the sky or the tall smooth tree trunks, with spirals of branches and their tufted foliage.

Two small bands of handsome bay horses, each with a bell-mare, water here. Often I hear from opposite directions the deep-toned music of their bells, against the sharper tinkle of the burro bell. No human comes to break the dreamy solitude. Far below, the tawny desert, seamed with canyons, throbs in the savage desert sun. But here it is lofty and cool.

It is hard not to be sentimental about my burros; they are such droll, friendly creatures. On the trail, particularly when they do the wrong thing in a tight place, I am often impatient with them, but when they stand up to their knees in wildflowers with blossoms in their lips, and look at me with their lustrous, large brown eyes, cocking their furry ears and switching their tails at their fat sides—then who that knew them could help loving them?

I had to laugh a few mornings ago on the desert, when tracking the two foolish-looking pals, I saw their trail leading up to an abandoned hogan and heard a snort and scuffle inside. With all the spacious desert around them, they had chosen to bed down in that little hogan, which just comfortably contained the two of them!

Wily burros, choosing "to bed down in that little hogan."

We followed a steep trail out of Cooper canyon opposite No Man's mesa. Near the rim it was just a scramble, and Leopard, whom I was packing, in attempting to claw his way over a steep place, lost his balance and fell over backwards. He turned two backward somersaults and a side roll, landing with his feet waving, about six inches from the yawning gulf. I pulled him to his feet. He was a bit groggy at first; he had lost a little fur, and the pack was scratched.

Now the moon swings clear the tree tops. The wind is in the pine trees; what other sound is like it?

The perfection of this place is one reason why I distrust ever returning to the cities. Here I wander in beauty and perfection. There one walks in the midst of ugliness and mistakes.

All is made for man but where can one find surroundings to match one's ideals and imaginings. It is possible to live and dream in ugly, ill-fitting places, but how much better to be where all is beautiful and unscarred.

With plenty of money, the way is smoothed, and it is fun to create a place to match your personality. Sometimes too it is fun to tinker away in a picturesque hovel, but the struggle for a mean existence is not worth it.

Here I take my belongings with me. The picturesque gear of packing, and my gorgeous Navajo saddleblankets, make a place my own. But when I go, I leave no trace.

The post where I last got my supplies is a costly place to trade. The owner has to haul his stuff 350 miles by truck, over the worst of roads. In this remote place he never sees a tourist, and seldom a dime crosses his counter in a year. All his business is trade, in wool, sheepskins, and blankets. Gallup, New Mexico is the nearest place where he can dispose of them. He has been offered 17 cents a pound for the wool which cost him 20 if he will haul it to New Mexico.

I baked a cake in my frying pan this noon. It was really a success. I wish you could have tasted it.

The beauty of this country is becoming a part of me. I feel more detached from life and somehow gentler. Except for passing flurries, it has become impossible for me to censure anyone.

[I wish harm to no one and occasionally try to be kind, though it seems futile striving. I have some good friends here, but no one who really understands why I am here or what I do. I don't know of anyone, though, who would have more than a partial understanding. I have gone too far alone.

I have always been unsatisfied with life as most people live it. Always I want to live more intensely and richly. Why muck and conceal one's true longings and loves, when by speaking of them one might find someone to understand them, and by acting on them one might discover oneself? It is true that in the world such lack of reserve usually meets with hostility, misunderstanding, and scorn. Here in isolation I need not fear on that score, although the strangers I do encounter usually judge me wrongly. But I was never one to be content with less than the most from life, and shall go on reaching, and leaving my soul defenseless to attacks. I seldom retaliate, for I perceive too well the ultimate futility.[81]]

Meanwhile I have used my body mercilessly, seldom giving way to it until forced, so that I should not wonder if it will turn traitor to me sometime. Anyway as Omar says, "If the soul can naked on the air of heaven ride, wer't not a shame for him in this clay carcass crippled to abide?" That is a big "if," but may the time never come when I have to minister to my body. [. . .]

Now the aspen trunks are tall and white in the moonlight. A wind croons in the pines. The mountain sleeps.

Peace to you,
Everett

Camp at Navajo Mountain...[82]

Letter to his parents from Navajo Mountain, Arizona, June 30, 1934

Dear Father and Mother:

The sun is beginning to set, and at last my camp is in shadow. The desert still throbs with heat, but below in the canyon frogs have begun to croak, heralding the cool approach of night. I am a day's journey from Rainbow bridge. Yesterday I came down the mountain, over a steep and rocky trail. The days on the mountain were delightful, and I cannot remember a more beautiful camp than the one I had there, under the tall pines and the aspens, with swarms of butterflies at the little trickling stream. [. . .]

Seen from the mountain, the country between here and the San Juan and Colorado rivers and beyond them is as rough and impenetrable a territory as I have ever seen. Thousands of domes and towers of sandstone lift their rounded pink tops from blue and purple shadows. To the east, great canyons seam the desert, cutting vermilion gashes through the grey green of the sage-topped mesas.

I remember well the tortuous trail leading out of Copper canyon opposite No Man's mesa. A vast expanse of broken country lay between the mesas. Far north was the silent, nearly empty canyon of the San Juan, with a vivid green strip of willows. Opposite me the mile-wide canyon was banded with blue green, grey blue, and delicate purple, surmounted by dull vermilion, which grew more vivid until at the rim of the mesa, the color was almost blindingly intense.

It has not rained for a whole month now, and most of the canyons and waterholes are dry. I have been lucky and diligent in my search for water. The burros have never had to go two days without it. Here there is fine clear water under cottonwoods. I enjoyed a splash this afternoon, and afterwards washed my shirt and socks.

The saffron of the clouds that lie low on the skyline is turning to soft blue grey. The orange turrets and pyramids opposite me fairly glow against the paling sky.

I reread "A Dreamer's Tales" of Dunsany on the mountain, and appreciated them more than ever. How beautifully Dunsany writes, and how rich his imagination is! I thoroughly sympathize with his hatred of the commercial, the ugly, and the unimaginative. [. . .]

I just reached Rainbow lodge tonight and found the people very friendly and likeable.

In the last two days I have traversed the longest continuous up-and-down broken trail that I ever went over. It was tremendously dramatic, to slide down steep sandhills in shadowed canyons only a dozen feet wide at the bottom, with towering walls above. I don't see how anyone was ever able to even plan the trail; there is such a maze of narrow winding canyons, many of them blocked at one end or both, and all buried down in the confusing jumble of towers and turrets, so that you can never see where they lead until you get there. It was a real thrill to go through that country.

I have just given the New York Times and the Manchester Guardian to Mrs. Wilson, and shall lend her one or two of my books. I have great pleasure in sharing things like that with people out here. I left the World Digests with Trader Dunn at Teece Ya Toh (Water under the cottonwoods).

Love from Everett

Here I Am Truly Alone ...[83]

Letter to a friend from Monument Valley, Utah, June, 1934

Dear X:

You could not guess in what a fantastic place I am. I sit in the shade of an ancient, dying juniper tree, cushioned on my Navajo saddle blankets. On all sides, the burning sun beats down on silent, empty desert. To right and left, long walls of sandstone mesas reach away into the distance, the shadows in their fluted clefts the color of claret. Before me the desert drops sheer away into a vast valley, in which strangely eroded buttes of all delicate and intense shadings of vermilion, orange and purple, tower into a cloudless turquoise sky.

Here I am truly alone. The faint tinkle of the bell of one of my burros is the only sound. The nearest water is many miles away.

This is near the end of a long trip—some 400 miles of desert, canyon and mountain. I have often thought of you, and regretted that something similar could not be happening to you. For I have had all and more than I ever desired. I have constantly known beauty so piercing as to be almost unbearable. I have led a wild gay life of fantastic adventures that seem to crowd upon me without my searching for them.

As a child I used to dream of such a life as this. Little did I imagine that all my dreams would be realized and all surpassed in every direction. Thinking of others, it has seemed almost wrong that one person should have such utter fulfillment while another leads a life of poisonous denial.

This time in my wanderings I have had more reckless self-confidence than ever before. I have gone my way regardless of everything but beauty. Trails I have used only when they went my way. Water I have discovered as I went, and remarkably enough, I have never been two days without finding it.

I know the Indians now—have lived with them and exchanged gifts, and enjoyed the hospitality of the finest of them, riding their horses and taking part in their ceremonies. I know the white people too—all the traders in this locality, and strange experiences I have had with them, but I like the Indians better. I had two true friends among the whites, but one was driven from the country by misfortune, and the other was killed a week ago. A truck lost a wheel and the load fell and crushed him.

Hundreds of times I have trusted my life to crumbling sandstone and nearly vertical angles in search for water or cliff dwellings. Twice I was nearly gored to death by a wild bull. But always so far I've escaped unscathed and gone on to other adventures.

Summer draws on; the shrill song of the cicadas is over, and the scarlet cactus blooms are gone. Columbine and sego lily have vanished too. Now only the sunflower and, in shaded canyons, the scarlet bugler are found. In these last few days the heat has been intense, and siestas have been in order. I have travelled only at dawn and evening, often after sunset, under the stars. I shall never forget coming down from the Lukachukai mountains at dusk, with the blood red moon falling through the pine branches as I descended.

Let me know how you are and what has happened.

Your good friend,
Everett

Excavating at Basket Maker Cave... [84]

Letter to his parents from Skeleton Mesa, Degosho Boko, Arizona, July 22, 1934

Dear Mother and Father:

At present I am in a cave below the rim of Skeleton Mesa, Arizona, looking out over the canyons of the Degosho Boko. This cave is in the Navajo sandstone a few feet under the rim. About three hundred feet below, and some 80 feet back under, is Twin

Caves cliff dwelling, but this cave is far more interesting. The culture here goes back to the first quarter of the Christian era, and presents many involved problems.

I have been in this locality about two weeks, working with the archaeological expedition. With me in the cave are an archaeologist, his assistant, and a photographer who also digs. Below in the canyon are ornithologists, entomologists, botanists, zoologists, geologists and the like, each with plenty of problems unsolved.

We have been in the cave for four days now. There is a very precarious way down the face of the cliff with footholds in stone, hundreds of years old. The only other way is the horse ladder, six miles up the canyon. We came that way with pack burros, passing the carcass of a horse that slipped. After two days wandering on the mesa top, in trackless forests, we crossed the bare rock ledges in a heavy cloudburst and came here.

We have found twelve burials here, with two fairly well preserved mummies. One mystery lies in the fact that all of the skeletons are headless, though there are some lower jaws. Evidently the graves were robbed—perhaps by the Pueblo people, but it is a difficult problem to ascertain the facts. There are traces of Basket Maker III and Pueblo I and II on the surface.

The Basket Makers are the oldest people who have been definitely traced back in the Southwest. They used the atlatl or throwing stick, and had corn. Pottery was first invented by the Pueblo I, and the bow came into use. Later beans and squash were used, and the turkey domesticated. In Pueblo II, pottery of a finer grade with different design types and color was used.

Twin Caves below is Pueblo III, with a further advance. In the whole Tsagi drainage there is no Pueblo IV. All the cliff dwellers were driven off by the eighteen-year drought that began in 1290.

I have been doing the packing and cooking here. Clayborn Lockett, the archaeologist in charge here, is a grizzled young chap of twenty-eight, widely experienced and a magnificent humorist. He is an ethnologist and something of an artist as well. His two helpers are boys of 19 and 20 from the University at Berkeley. We have great fun up here by ourselves, discovering something new every day, and looking out over everything from our sheltered cave.

I am working on a black-and-white of my outfit, wheeling about on the floor of the Canyon del Muerto, under looming shadowy cliffs, at dusk.[85]

Love from Everett

Tsegi Canyon

I Almost Lost One Burro...[86]

Letter to Waldo from Kayenta, Arizona, August 19, 1934

Dear Waldo:

Your letter of July 17 reached me about a week ago at Skeleton mesa. As you know, I was with the expedition for some time, assisting in the archaeological work. It was most fascinating, working in high vaulted caves far above the lonely canyons. The last night's work was done by firelight. Huge shadows played on the orange wall of the cave, which reaches upwards into the darkness. Outside, rain hissed down, and once we heard wild geese honking as they flew south. The last job was sawing beams and sticks for tree-ring data, to establish the dates. We have one date already—1127 A.D. The cave I worked in before was about 500 A.D. but the tree ring calendar has not been pushed back that far.

I managed to sell a few pictures while I was with the group, and then I left it to follow a dramatic trail over the Comb ridge. I stopped at White Dog cave, where an enormous sandstone block fell down and crushed the inhabitants at their work, some hundreds of years ago. Two dogs were found with them. I found a white arrowhead there myself.

Yesterday I went for a ride through Monument valley with a friend of mine who paints, and we had a great day, winding up with a swim in Kayenta creek. This afternoon I am starting for Black mesa. I intend to cross it and reach Hotevilla in the Hopi country in time for the snake dance.

Monument Valley

I have seen more wild country than on any previous trip. I almost lost one burro in the quicksands—he was up to his neck—and the other fell over backward in trying to climb a cliff. I myself had endless difficult climbs and descents—like one time when three of us came down a cliff by moonlight, using old worn-out hand holds. Yesterday morning I found a big centipede in my pack. When I walked to Rainbow bridge[87] at night I found a six-inch scorpion beside my bed at dawn. I have been working away, painting, but I get exhausted and discouraged at times. This is certainly magnificent country, not easy to paint.

My plans are not definite, but I think I shall go to the Grand Canyon from the Hopi country, and maybe spend the winter exploring around Thunder river or the Kaiparowitz plateau and Straight cliffs.

I hope you have a good trip North.

Love from Everett

At the Hopi Ceremonial Dance...[88]

Cards to his parents from Gallup in August and September, 1934

August 29, 1934
Gallup, New Mexico

Dear Mother:

I rode here from Second mesa with a Hopi silversmith, who was selling turquoise along the way. Vernon and I spent a night in a Hopi kiva at Mishongnovi, watching Indians practice the Buffalo and Antelope dances. Now we are going to see some of the dances at the Inter-tribal Indian ceremonial. Yesterday I sent you a Hopi bowl from Hotevilla.

Love from Everett
[Image on postal card: Navajo blanket weaver and papoose.]

September 1, 1934
Gallup, New Mexico

Dear Mother:

I'm starting back for Second Mesa with some Hopi today. My friend and I have been learning Indian songs. I got a fine blanket for my saddle. How do you like these San Domingo women?

Love from Everett
[Image on postal card: Indian ceremonial by San Domingo women.]

I Danced with the Hopi...[89]

Card to his parents from Grand Canyon in September, 1934

Dear Father and Mother:

Arrived here at Desert View last night. Found your combined letter today, about your own trip north. Lost a burro (Leopard) down little Colorado canyon the other day, with some of the pack, but have already replaced him with a bigger burro. My camp is next to that of an artist from Tahiti. Since Gallup I have been at Mishongnovi, where my Hopi friends painted me up and had me in their Antelope dance. I was the only white person there. Killed two rattlers the other day. One struck before I saw him. I caught the other alive. Sold a print yesterday.

Love from Everett

I Drove Away Evil Spirits ... [90]

Letter to Ned Frisius from Flagstaff, Arizona, September 27, 1934

Dear Ned:

I was surprised and pleased to find your letter at Grand Canyon the other day. I have spent the past week near Flagstaff vacationing. I left my burros, Cockleburrs and Chocolatero, under the care of an artist friend at Desert View, and took the highway down here to visit a friend with whom I did some archaeological work this summer. It was fascinating work—in ruins dating from eight hundred to 15 hundred years back. And the climbing—up almost sheer sandstone cliffs, clinging by worn footholds hundreds of years old, or on narrow crumbling edges—was more spectacular than anything in the Sierras.

From Flagstaff I went south to Oak creek, and painted some brilliantly lighted vermilion cliffs against inky storm skies. I came back and saw the first snows on the San Francisco peaks, and the slopes golden with yellowing aspens.

Evidently you overheard something of my adventure with my friends the Indians. I have a great time with them, especially the Navajos. I once spent three days far up a desert canyon, assisting and watching a Navajo "sing" for a sick woman. I drove away countless hordes of evil spirits but after I went away the girl died. The sand paintings, seldom seen by white men, were gorgeous.

In my wanderings this year, I have taken more chances and had more and wilder adventures than ever before. And what magnificent country I have seen—wild, tremendous wasteland stretches, lost mesas, blue mountains rearing upward from the vermilion sands of the desert, canyons five feet wide at the bottom and hundreds of feet deep, cloudbursts roaring down unnamed canyons, and hundreds of houses of the cliff dwellers, abandoned a thousand years ago.

Glad you are getting a good start at college.

Your friend,
Everett

Fascinating ruins, "dating from eight hundred to 15 hundred years back"

Heading Across the Pink Cliffs ...[91]

Letter to his parents from Tropic, Utah, November, 1934

Dear Father and Mother:

I have been having great fun here today with a Mormon family. There are nine children, and the father is a ranger in Bryce canyon. This morning I rode out with one of the boys to look for a cow. We rode all over the hills, and stopped at an orchard to load up with apples. Then I went to church, my first time in a Mormon church. It was an interesting experience, and about my first time in church since I was in San Francisco. In our class we had quite a talk about crime, economics, juvenile court, etc. A frank discussion of the national crisis. One of them said that the war and turmoil prophecies of one of their Mormon saints would be fulfilled next year.

A while ago I sold a couple of pictures to Charlie Plumb, Ella Cinders cartoonist, who owns a ranch in a dramatic situation at Cave lakes. [. . .]

I enjoyed riding down from Bryce canyon through the grotesque and colorful formation. Mother would surely enjoy the trees; they are fascinating, especially the twisted little pines and junipers. I had never seen the foxtail pine before. It is a ridiculous caricature of a tree, with gangling limbs and most amusing foxtails lopping out in all directions, with no symmetry at all. There is a natural bridge called Tower bridge.

Hotevilla is a modern Hopi pueblo, founded in 1908 as the result of a bitter quarrel in Oraibi, concerning the old and the new way. Oraibi is said to be the oldest continuously inhabited place in America—seven hundred years, I think. It was left almost deserted after the quarrel. My painting is of some end houses on the rim of the mesa, near the snake kiva.

The Hopi woman in the upper right house makes pottery canteens and for some superstitious reason, always two at once. They hang mutton jerky out to dry. They did not like me to paint the old man, but I pacified them. [. . .]

The weather has mostly been delightful, although I was in one snow flurry on the Paunsagunt plateau. Now I am heading across the pink cliffs toward Escalante and the lower country toward the river.

Love from Everett

P.S. Later in the day we had more fun—apple fights, church, and until about morning we amused ourselves with some Navajos who were camped nearby.

Tomorrow I Take the Trail Again ... [92]

Letter to his parents from Escalante, Utah, November 11, 1934. This was the last letter written by Everett Ruess, so far as is known.[93]

Dear Father and Mother:

After a truly delightful trip over the mountains, finding my way without any trails, I have reached the Mormon town of Escalante. [. . .] I am going south towards the river now, through some rather wild country. I am not sure yet whether I will go across Smoky mountain to Lee's ferry and south, or whether I will try to cross the river above the San Juan. The water is very low this year. I might even come back through Boulder. So I may not have a post office for a couple of months. I am taking an ample supply of food with me.

I have had plenty of fun with the boys of this town, riding horses, hunting for arrowheads, and the like. I took a couple of boys to the show last night—"Death Takes a Holiday." I liked it as well as the play, enjoying the music especially. This year the *pinon* nut crop is unusual, and every one occupies his leisure time in eating them. This year the severe drought and the grasshoppers have made a critical situation for the farmers.

I promised you some pictures and I am sending a few[94] of them now, as it will lighten the load, and they are getting travel-stained. They all have faults, but those I like best, and mean to frame for my room later, are Betatakin, Ghost Cedars, The Pinnacle, Desert Light,[95] Ahgahashluh, and Desert Noon.

I have sold away a few more lately, but I hope you will like those I am sending. As I have more money than I need now, I am sending you $10, and I want each of you to spend five for something you have been wishing to have—books, or a trip, but not anything connected with any kind of a duty. Let this be the first installment on that nickel I promised you when I made my first million.

I'm also enclosing a couple of clippings which I thought would amuse you. The one about Dwight Morrow made me think of Father.

Tonight I have been sitting by the fire with two of my friends, eating roast venison and baked potatoes. The burro bell is tinkling merrily nearby as Chocolatero crops the alfalfa. He is a good burro now. It was hard to get him across the Colorado river suspension bridge, as he was very frightened by it. A packer dragged him across behind his mule, and he left a bloody track all the way across. Later it was hard to teach him to make the fordings where the water was deep and swift, but now he does not mind. I took the burros' shoes off yesterday.

So, tomorrow I take the trail again, to the canyons south.

Love from Everett

I Have Not Tired of the Wilderness . . . [96]

Letter to Waldo from Escalante, Utah, November, 1934. This was the last letter written to his brother before he disappeared in the Utah wilderness.

Dear Waldo:

[. . .] As to when I shall revisit civilization, it will not be soon, I think. I have not tired of the wilderness; rather I enjoy its beauty and the vagrant life I lead more keenly all the time. I prefer the saddle to the street car, and the star-sprinkled sky to the roof, the obscure and difficult trail leading into the unknown to any paved highway, and the deep peace of the wild to the discontent bred by cities. Do you blame me then for staying here where I feel that I belong and am one with the world about me? It is true that I miss intelligent companionship, but there are so few with whom I can share the things that mean much to me that I have learned to contain myself. It is enough that I am surrounded with beauty and carry it with me in things that are a constant delight, like my gorgeous Navajo saddle blankets and the silver bracelet on my wrist, whose three turquoises gleam in the firelight.[97] [. . .]

A few days ago I rode into the red rocks and sandy desert, and it was like coming home again. I even met a couple of wandering Navajos, and we stayed up most of the night talking, eating roast mutton with black coffee, and singing songs. The songs of the Navajo express for me something that no other songs do. And now that I know enough of it, it is a real delight to speak in another language.

I have not seen a human being nor any wild life but squirrels and birds for two or three days. Yesterday was a loss as far as travel was concerned, for I got into an impasse in the head of a canyon system, and had to return to where I started. Last night I camped under tall pines by a stream that flowed under a towering orange cliff, like a wall against the sky, dwarfing the twisted pines on its summit and the tall straight ones that grow part way up the face of it. It was glorious at sunrise. Today I have ridden over miles of rough country, forcing my way through tall sage and stubborn oak brush, and driving the burros down canyon slopes so steep that they could hardly keep from falling. At last I found a trail, and have just left it to make dry camp on what seems like the rim of the world. My camp is on the very point of the divide, with country falling away to the blue horizon on east and west. The last rays of the sun at evening, and the first at dawn reach me. Below are steep cliffs where the canyon has cut its way up to the rim of the divide. Northward is the sheer face of Mount Kaiparowitz, pale vermilion capped with white, with a forested summit. West and south are desert and distant mountains. Tonight the pale crescent of new moon appeared for a little while, low on the skyline, at sunset. [. . .]

[. . .] This has been a full, rich year. I have left no strange or delightful thing undone that I wanted to do. [. . .]

Affectionately,
Everett

"What Became of Everett Ruess?…" [98]
by Hugh Lacy

"NEMO." After five years that cryptic clue seems to summarize the desert mystery of Everett Ruess, young Los Angeles artist-adventurer who disappeared at 20 in the wasteland of Southeastern Utah, last seen in November 1934.

"Nemo" is Latin for no one.

That word, inscribed on the walls of a cave and again a mile away on the doorstep of an old Moqui Indian house, was found in June 1935, during the second search for Everett, conducted by the Associated civic clubs of southern Utah. Captain P. M. Shurtz of Escalante, Utah, led a dozen men in a 10-day quest, locating what may have been Everett's last camp near Davis canyon.

There with the remains of a fire, the date of "1934" and the enigmatic "Nemo" carved with a knife, the trail ended.

Everett left Escalante to write and paint among the cliff dwellings. A sheep man, Clayton Porter, on November 19, saw him last near where Escalante creek enters the Colorado.

Everett deplored the defacing of natural scenery, yet all evidence indicates that the young artist carved the words and date. And if he did mark "Nemo" on the walls, it was probably an unconscious act—and may be a key to his thoughts and to the riddle of his vanishing.

It was not unusual for Everett Ruess to leave home. Since his first scout camping trip at 13 Everett's sojourns in the wild were periodic. The summers of 1930 and '33 he spent in Sequoia and Yosemite parks, and in the High Sierra, the summers of '31 and '32 in the Southwest. It was just another summer's outing when he left for the Southwest desert for the third time, April 12, 1934. His brother Waldo drove him in Waldo's Ford from Los Angeles to Kayenta, Arizona. Such was the outset of Everett's fifth—and last—major trip from home.

From Kayenta through Gallup, New Mexico, to Grand Canyon, Zion park and Bryce park he traveled in the fall of 1934, to Escalante, Utah. From there he set out November 11 [12], 1934. His letters said he would be out of touch with parents and friends for "about two months," but did not definitely indicate his plans. He "might" live awhile among the Indians near Navajo mountain. He had met Navajo along the way—wandering sheep men—in Tropic and Escalante. He spoke their tongue. He "might" go down along the river to Marble canyon, or else "come back by way of Boulder." It was later learned from John Wetherill of Kayenta, who with a map helped Everett chart his journey, that his trip was to have ended at Wilson's mesa not far from Navajo mountain where he might find interesting cliff dwellings to paint.

On other trips to the desert Everett had often written that he would be out of communication for three or four weeks. Other than these intervals his carefully-phrased letters were faithfully written. Everett's parents waited two months as Everett had directed. They hesitated to begin inquiries—Everett was sensitive of concern about him. Then, February 7, 1935, they wrote to the postmistress at Escalante, Mrs. H. J. Allen. Letters followed to the postmasters at all the towns and cities of the Southwest which Everett had visited. They wrote to the sheriffs in all the counties he had passed through, to the Indian agents, forestry and conservation officials, newspapers, radio stations, and to all individuals he had mentioned in his letters.

The first news story of his disappearance appeared in the Los Angeles Evening Herald February 14. A reporter in Arizona picked up the story when a forestry man showed him a letter from the parents. Many news stories followed in Los Angeles, later in Associated and United Press dispatches over the country as the searches proceeded.

The parents, by February 26, felt from the many replies to their letters that Everett must be secure. All correspondents said that he was trail-wise, experienced, capable of looking out for himself, probably entirely safe.

Indian Trackers on Trail

On February 28 Captain Neal Johnson, placer miner of Hanksville, Utah, having learned from Mrs. Florence Lowery of Marble Canyon, Utah [Arizona] of Everett's disappearance called at the Ruess home in Los Angeles. He proposed hiring three Navajo to search the Navajo mountain country. The Ruesses subsidized this expedition. They heard vague reports from Indians through Captain Johnson over a period of many weeks. Nothing came of the search.

On March 3, H. J. Allen of Escalante communicated with the Ruesses and offered to conduct a search with the aid of Escalante men, saying, "We will search for him as though he were our own son." Ten or a dozen men covered 70 or 80 square miles in the neighborhood of Davis canyon near where Escalante creek enters the Colorado in southeastern Utah. On March 7 Everett's two burros were found in Davis canyon. In a cave in the same area prints of his number nine boots were found, and a heap of choice shards he had gathered. Nothing else was found.

The burros were in a natural corral large enough in good season for several months' grazing, but the weather was backward and they were thin and starved.[99] Their halters had been found weeks before, it later appeared, by an Escalantan who thought nothing of their significance.

The March 9 entry in Mr. Ruess' diary gives the opinion that Everett was probably snowed in for the winter. Everett had prepared himself with $30 worth of provisions from two general stores in Escalante before starting.

On March 12 Bill Jacobs of Hollywood turned over to the parents 30 letters he had received from Everett revealing much of the lad's innermost thoughts and nature. As time went on other friends over the country sent the parents letters received from their son.

March 28 was Everett's 21st birthday.

By April 8 the parents were led to believe by communications from Captain Johnson and others that Everett had crossed the Colorado river and was safe with the Indians, perhaps retreating from the lands and life of the pale-face.

April 28, following a communication from their friend Judge Ben Lindsey to Secretary of War Dern in Washington, D.C., the parents went to March Field and conferred with General Arnold who, however, scouted the idea that government or other airplanes would be able to locate such a small object as Everett's camp in the cliff and canyon-broken country where low flying was impracticable.

Sleepy burro, taking it easy during the heat of the day.

Last Camp Is Found

The people of southern Utah did not wish to believe that in their part of the world anybody could vanish into thin air. The Associated civic clubs of southern Utah representing 15 counties equipped another expedition of a dozen men who spent about 10 days following June 1 in a search. They covered much the same country under the leadership of Captain P. M. Shurtz as did the party under H. J. Allen. This experience revealed what is believed to be Everett's last camp in a cave near Davis canyon, and the carved "Nemo, 1934," marked on the cave walls and again a mile away on the doorstep of a Moqui Indian house. A long-distance telephone call was made to the Ruesses in Los Angeles to learn the meaning and possible significance of "Nemo." This expedition was given daily coverage by the Salt Lake Tribune. Joe Larson, a member of the party, each day took a report of the progress made to a point from which he could communicate with Ray Carter, secretary of the Associated civic clubs, and correspondent of the Tribune.

In the hope of producing some new clue Mr. and Mrs. Ruess decided June 22 on a trip through the country Everett traversed to meet personally the people he had known and with whom he corresponded. On their 2400-mile trip they visited friends of his at Grand Canyon; Kayenta, where they met Mr. and Mrs. John Wetherill; Cameron and Tuba City; Marble Canyon, where they met Mr. and Mrs. Buck Lowery; Zion park, where they met Chief Ranger and Mrs. Donal J. Jolly; Bryce park, meeting Chief Ranger and Mrs. Maurice Cope; and Tropic, meeting George D. Shakespeare. At Panguitch, Utah, they met President Frank Martines, Secretary Ray Carter and other members of the Associated civic clubs of southern Utah. At Escalante they visited the Allens, meeting many of the searchers of the two expeditions, including Walt Allen, Gene Bailey, Harvey Bailey, Frank Barney, Loren Blood, George Davis, Claude Haws, Joe Larson, Chester Lay, Alden Moyes, Oris Moyes, Ronald Schow, Alton Twitchell, Earl Woolsey, Jack Woolsey, Prudencio Zabala, Will R. Barker, Joe Predenzo, Hugh Chestnut, L. C. Christensen and Eldrid Mitchell.

July 13 the parents communicated with the sheriff at Gallup, New Mexico, regarding a skeleton found burned in the desert near Gallup. Dental evidence disclosed that it could not have been Everett.

About July 29 letters were received suggesting that Everett might be living in disguise in Blanding, Utah. This proved to be an error.

In August, inspired by Captain Neal Johnson who still insisted that Everett might be living with the Indians near Navajo mountain, the Salt Lake Tribune sent Captain Johnson with one of their star reporters, John U. Terrel, discoverer of the spectacles that led to the solution of the Chicago Leopold-Loeb murder case. The 11-day trip was given full-page illustrated stories in the Tribune, and led to the hint that Everett had been murdered for his outfit. It was suggested that the state of Utah equip and conduct an expedition at the request of the counties in which Everett was last seen. Citizens of some counties, in which a murder had not been committed in half a century resented and scoffed at the suggestion. Nothing further was done.

Letters, clues and hints since that time have been investigated by the Ruess family with no helpful results. One of the chief among these was the experience of Mr. and Mrs. MacAntire of Los Angeles who saw a young man they believed later to be Everett near Moab, Utah, February, 1937.

The Ruesses are not inclined to follow occult investigations, but friends have consulted mediums and psychics from California to Massachusetts. Some seers said that he was safe with the Indians. Others said that he had been drowned crossing the Colorado on a crudely-constructed raft. Others merely said that he was dead. None said that he was murdered. None said that he fell, suffered amnesia, and still lives and travels unaware of his identity. Parents and friends, of course, have seen Everett in dreams, alike contradictory—living, dead, among the Indians, or, as the parents occasionally dream, trudging up to the backdoor, dumping his heavy outfit, saying, "Well, here I am!"

John Wetherill of Kayenta, who helped Everett chart his last trip, agrees with the opinion of most Escalante folk that Everett fell from some high cliff dwelling and that his outfit, covered by blowing sand, may be found only by accident years hence. Mr. Syrett of Ruby's Inn near the entrance to Bryce park, to whom Everett disclosed a desire to live with the Indians for a time, said that if Everett had fallen to his death in the dry desert atmosphere near Davis canyon his body would mummify where it fell, and that carrion birds would not come to it. The cliffs are so numerous and abrupt that with rope and ladder it would be a tremendous task to investigate them. Twenty years or so hence when the district in which Everett disappeared may become a national monument or park, some one may stumble upon Everett's last diary of 1934 with his best writing in it and upon some of his last and choicest water-colors, as well as the Navajo bracelet, "whose three turquoises gleam in the firelight."

Of Everett's risks H. C. Lockett, the archaeologist in Everett's letter "With Archaeologists at Basket Maker Cave," writes, "I had an excellent chance really to know Everett . . . he spent much of his time in this burial cave with me . . . we had many talks together and I know that Everett was always anxious to get into situations which provided thrills and excitement. When these situations arose he would think about them, write about them or often paint them. One time in camp he stood on the edge of a 400-foot cliff during a rainstorm and did a water-color sketch of a waterfall. I remember this very clearly because I personally was scared to death just watching him perched on the edge of the cliff. It is my idea that some place while climbing a cliff . . . he may possibly have fallen to his death . . . I have read with interest the accounts in the Desert Magazine."

And so in the dilemma of Everett Ruess conjectures swing from one horn to the other, from the easily conceivable wilderness death that his writings seemed to portend, to the life of wandering and renunciation symbolized in a word.

The recurring supposition of Everett's being alive is not based alone on an artist's moods, and on passages from his works suggestive of self-exile. He was capable of making his own way. Six months before his disappearance he asked that his monthly "stipend" be cut in half, and in his last letter he sent his parents a gift of ten dollars. In the last month he wrote, "I sold a couple of pictures to Charlie Plumb, the Ella Cinders cartoonist, who owns a ranch in a dramatic situation . . ." He may have felt that his parents were of philosophic nature and would understand his need to pursue the unknown.

Reports have come from time to time of young men alone in the desert, any one of whom might have been young Ruess.

In February 1937, Mr. and Mrs. Arthur MacAntire, vacationers in Utah, saw at a mining site near Moab a young man they later believed, on learning of the case, to be Everett. Attracted by the picturesque man, Mrs. MacAntire approached him, wanting to converse, but was abruptly rebuffed. This, the only unfriendly occurrence of her tour, impressed his features upon her. She identified pictures of Everett later in Los Angeles as being the youth she saw. Unwillingness to talk could be attributed to the California license, and to Everett's preference to remain "undiscovered."

Numerous theories have been propounded. Readers of the Desert Magazine have volunteered information. But the riddle is still unsolved—as unreadable as the wilderness that swallowed him. Perhaps Everett, for whom "the lone trail was the best" gave the only answer three years before his final departure—"In the meanwhile, my burro and I, and my little dog, if I can find one, are going on and on, until, sooner of later, we reach the end of the horizon."

Appendix

"Is Everett Ruess in Mexico?"
by Cora L. Keagle [100]

On the ninth of April, 1937, my husband and I were returning from a jaunt to Mexico City. Nine miles south of Monterrey, we saw two young fellows tinkering with the motor of an old car stalled by the roadside.

In Mexico, where there is leisure for civilities, everyone stops to render assistance when cars misbehave so we remembered our manners and pulled up opposite the car.

It seemed the owner of the complaining car had purchased a new jet for the carburetor in Monterey but it had proved to be the wrong size, so the car, after wheezing along for nine miles, had given a final gasp and stopped. No amount of tinkering produced more than a cough from the motor so the owner suggested that his passenger ride on to Monterrey with us, exchange the jet and catch a ride back while he stayed with the car. And so it was arranged.

The young fellow came over to us, then saying, "Just a minute," returned for his portfolio. "I never let this out of sight. It's the source of my living," he remarked, and put the portfolio in our car.

"That sounds interesting," I ventured. Then he explained that he did water colors and was always able to make his way by selling them or exchanging them for food and lodgings.

In the few minutes it took to drive to Monterrey he asked many questions about Mexico City. A cousin of ours in the back seat happened to mention Chicago. He told her that he had studied art in Chicago, also said he had been living among the Indians in Arizona painting and writing. Being interested in art I remembered this part of the conversation especially.

At Monterrey he thanked us for the ride and we parted in the casual way of chance travelers but there was something about his personality that made us remember him definitely.

At that time we had never heard of Everett Ruess but when the September issue of Desert Magazine came out and I read Mr. Lacy's story[101] I was instantly convinced that he was the young artist who had ridden with us to Monterrey. There was the likeness of the photograph, the fact that he had painted in Arizona and that he painted in water colors.

I couldn't wait to show the illustration to Mr. Keagle, so I ran out to the cactus garden where he was working and asked him if he still remembered the face of the young artist we picked up in Mexico. When he said he remembered him well, I showed the illustration. He looked at it a minute then exclaimed, "That's the very fellow."

We are convinced that we saw Everett Ruess. True, it was two years and six months after he disappeared but the Saltillo region out of Monterrey is a remote place very interesting to artists so it is quite conceivable that he had been in Mexico for some time.

And if it was Everett he was tanned, healthy and happy and several pounds heavier than when he disappeared.

Letter from Tad Nichols [102]

Rt. 2, Box 194
Tucson, Arizona

To Desert Magazine Editor:

In the April [1939] issue of the Desert Magazine I was much interested to read the letter by Everett Ruess.[103] Randolph Jenks and I were the "two boys" he mentions who loaded his burro on a truck and took him to Flagstaff. The enclosed photo was taken on that day in June, 1931.

*Everett (left) and Randolph Jenks, loading Ruess's burro
into the back of the pick-up truck.*

Jenks and I were returning from a trip to Lees Ferry bridge. About five miles north of Cameron, while bumping along the old road, we came upon a boy and a burro, slowly moving over the white, glaring sand. It was hot and dusty that day, and we stopped and asked the boy if he would like a drink. He must have thought at first we were asking for water, for he started to unlash one of his two canteens from the side of the burro. He had very little water, but was immediately willing to share it with others.

After gratefully drinking from our canteen, the boy talked to us, and we soon learned his name was Everett. He had been on a walking trip all through Del Muerto and De Chelly canyons, a region we had always wanted to see. By plying him with questions, we learned of the many cliff dwellings he had seen, and of his precarious climbs to some high isolated ones.

"I know that many of the cliff houses which I reached," said Everett, "must never have been visited before by white men. In one I found a cradleboard in perfect condition, together with many pieces of fine cloth."

We became much interested in Everett and his stories, and before long he produced some paintings which he had made during his De Chelly trip. One water color, that of the White House Ruin, was exceptionally good, and Jenks offered to purchase it, asking Everett the price he received for his work. I remember his reply: "Well, a day laborer gets about fifty cents an hour, and it must have taken me about three hours to do the painting!"

Everett looked a little hot and tired, so we decided to take him up to our ranch, situated at 8000 feet on the side of the San Francisco peaks. At first we feared, after unsuccessful pulling and pushing, that we would not be able to get the burro into the back of the pick-up truck. Finally we backed the Ford up against the embankment of Highway 89, which at that time was just being graded. With the road on a level with the floor of the truck, we were able to lead the burro aboard. We tied him with ropes hooked to the sides of the truck, and roped our bedrolls and camping outfit to the roof of the cab. The three of us, together with Curly, then piled into the car, and started the last 60 miles into town. It must have been a comical sight to see us arrive in Flagstaff that evening.

After one night at Mesa Ranch School Camp, we took Everett to Deerwater Ranch, where he remained for several days, working on paintings of the Aspen trees. As I remember, he then left for the Grand Canyon, and I heard no more of his whereabouts until I saw a notice in the paper that he was lost in Utah. Everett had a true love of the desert, an enthusiasm for remote, lonely, and inaccessible canyons, which to him were the most fascinating.

Sincerely yours,
Tad Nichols

"Who Was 'Nemo'?"

Los Angeles, California
January, 1940

Editor, Desert Magazine:

The article about our son Everett Ruess in the December [1939] Desert Magazine[104] leaves unanswered the possible meaning of the world "Nemo" that Everett carved in the cave and on the doorstep of the Moqui Indian House. In all probability it is an echo from repeated reading of Jules Verne's "Twenty Thousand Leagues Under the Sea." Everett's copy is well worn. Captain Nemo, hero of the novel, long years before the modern submarine was invented, deserted civilization, invented a new language, enlisted a crew, and traveled in a submarine, scientist that he was, joyously exploring the flora and fauna of the seven seas.

Everett's letters, essays and diaries indicate in many hints that he felt modern cities to be "big mistakes." Against the artificial in excess he revolted. Art and artists, he felt, should be subsidized, not commercialized. It would not be impossible that he desired to die to the world, as it were, and be reincarnated in a still freer life, all in one life-time.

Whether Everett is alive or dead, he is at peace now. He left us and the world in 20 years more to remember and to treasure than could be required of an average hundred years. We have released him in our hearts to steer by the North Star of his own soul. Even were he found alive, we would have no desire to interfere with his fulfilment of his life and destiny.

Christopher G. Ruess

P.S. There is another interpretation of "Nemo" that has occurred to some of Everett's friends. It hints at the conclusion that Everett met his end trying to ferry himself and his goods and gear across the Colorado in a home-made raft, near where the Escalante creek enters the Colorado river, at or near Hole-in-the-wall. The "Astrological Bulletina," Los Angeles, Calif., for Autumn, 1937, contains an article, "The Art of Synthesis," for astrologers by Leigh Hope Milburn, of nine pages, finding that his horoscope indicated death by water.

Everett had read much of Lawrence of Arabia, man of the desert, who won the Moslem for Britain and the allies in the first world war. Especially he read Lawrence's translation of the Odyssey of Homer, the earliest novel. In this is the story of "Nemo," Latin for "Odysseus," or "Oudeis," meaning "No One." Odysseus is captured by the one-eyed giant Polyphemus and imprisoned in the giant's cave. Odysseus puts the giant's lone eye out with a burning stick. The giant howls with pain. His crew come near and ask, "What is the matter?" "No One has put my eye out," cries Polyphemus. His crew laugh at his yells, saying, "Why rave about what No One has done!" Odysseus escapes by tying himself underneath one of the shaggy sheep kept by Polyphemus in the cave at night and released by day to feed. Then Odysseus crosses the wild water between Italy and the land where the anthropophagi or man-eating savages live, just as Everett, having been in the caves where he carved "Nemo" intended to cross the Colorado to live with the Navajo for a while. Polyphemus threw great rocks at the fleeing Odysseus, which missed their mark, but became great islands nevertheless. Everett may have been playing that he was again "Nemo" or "Oudesi" or "No One," except that Everett did not succeed in crossing the raging waters.[105]

Letter from Lawrence Janssens[106]

Brooklyn, New York

Editor, Desert Magazine:

I am writing you to let you know how much I like your Desert Magazine. As an interpretation and appreciation of the beauty and fascination of the Southwest it is wonderful. I have enjoyed every issue of the magazine I have read, literally from cover to cover. It makes me long to be back in the country through which I used to camp years ago, for the loveliness of desert dawns and sunsets, and the gaunt grotesqueness of rock masses and Joshua trees.

Your printing of the letters of Everett Ruess is particularly interesting to me because we were schoolmates and friends, and because we shared camping trips together many times before our ways digressed. I still treasure his letters which told of his enjoyment of the desert and mountain country we both loved. He was a rare spirit in this world of dull clods, and his disappearance caused me great sadness, but it can always be said of him that he, of all people, really found the happiness for which he sought, that he really lived during his desert wanderings, drank of the beauty and grandeur of that wild country.

But why don't you print more of his artistic works as well as his letters? He was equally remarkable for the spirit of the desert which he infused in his brush and pencil, and block prints such as you had in your April issue or reproductions of his paintings would supplement his writings.

Wishing every kind of success both for you and for the Desert Magazine, that the loveliness of the Southwest be learned and appreciated by more people than ever.

Lawrence Janssens

Note: Lawrence and his mother took Everett on many week-end trips. After her death, Lawrence went to sea in order to have time for writing. He attained the rank of first mate on a freighter, and married a Brooklyn girl, still continuing with his novel and plays. In the great Atlantic storm, February, 1940, Laurence met a tragic fate, being swept off the deck of his ship. His body was not recovered.

"Everett's Home"

Everett's mother is Stella Knight Ruess. She is an artist of versatility, her work including block prints, bookplates, carving and modeling. Booklets she has produced include "Star Glints," "Poems in Trees," "In the Red Flame" for Campfire Girls, and "Los Angeles in Blackprint." She illustrated "Quaker Bonnets" for Sara Bundy Pence, and edited "Words of Wisdom" for Sunset Hall. With Alfred and Emerson Knight she edited "William Henry Knight, California Pioneer," written of her father by Bertha Knight Power. She is a member of the National League of American Pen Women.[107]

Christopher Ruess, Everett's father, is a California pioneer in probation work. He is a Harvard graduate and formerly was chief probation officer at Oakland, California. For several years he has been a member of the probation department of Los Angeles County. Mr. Ruess was for a short time in the ministry of Unitarian churches at Alameda and Fresno, California. He was also for 10 years or so in business as sales manager in Boston and New York, with work in many other states and in Canada.[108]

Everett's older brother, Waldo, was working as a secretary for the Metropolitan Water District of Los Angeles in the desert at Berdoo Camp during much of the time that Everett was in the desert. He has since been in China several years with the

National Chinese Christian Council at Shanghai, the Dupont Company at Hankow, and latterly with the American Embassy at Tokyo, Japan, and at this writing with American Ambassador Johnson at Chungking, China.

The present Ruess home at 531 N. Ardmore Ave., Los Angeles, reflects the artistic tastes of the occupants. The moderate-sized garden has a woodsy, oriental atmosphere, with a cypress tree, an escallonia tree, a fish pool, a tea-house and a background of golden bamboo. It has been a setting for poetic programs for various groups and clubs. During the Christmas season Mrs. Ruess' collection of Madonna figurines has been exhibited for friends in all parts of the house and in unexpected garden nooks.

Everett's poems and letters in this volume were written in 1929 and later through 1934, during the deepest years of the great depression. The business in which his father was employed for many years failed about 1928 and Mr. Ruess returned to his old profession of probation work in 1930. On January 27, 1934, from San Francisco Everett wrote to his father: "What you say is partly true, in your remark that I have done what I most wanted to do in spite of the world crisis. Today I found three letters from friends in various quarters of whom it is by no means true. They have been wallowing in the shallows of life this past year—not growing nor having new and enlarging experiences, driven partly or wholly by circumstances into lives that they themselves consider ignoble, stale, and depressing."

Everett had all the advantages of an intelligent and understanding home in modest financial circumstances. He loved his home and family. His letters are proof of that. To those who may wonder why he should leave such a home to follow the remote desert trails for long periods at a time, it may only be suggested that in every human heart there is more or less unconscious yearning for the freedom that is to be found only in close association with Nature—away from the restrictions imposed by a more or less artificial society. To an imaginative mind these bonds become highly oppressive at times.

Everett Ruess differed from others of his highly artistic temperament only in the fact that he had the opportunity and the courage and will to go forth and seek the realization of his dreams.

In a letter written home in 1934 he said of himself: "I have three million-dollar endowments that I am sure of, and I don't have to go begging. I have my very deep sensitivities to beauty, to music, and to nature. In addition, thanks to you and to mother, I have an intellect that is capable of analysis and of grappling with things almost anywhere I turn. I do not regret my freedom. On all sides I meet people who are not able to follow things up as I am doing, and it is not I who envy them."

Randall Henderson

Note: Everett's parents would be glad to hear through the publisher from others who have interesting letters from Everett, which they would like to see and copy and return. As Everett probably sold his best watercolors, they would be pleased to hear from any readers who own watercolors by Everett.

Everett Ruess Awards

A small insurance policy on Everett's life has been turned into an annuity on the lives of his parents. As long as either of them live, from time to time as funds accumulate, boys and girls of the Southwestern states that Everett traversed will be invited to excel in one or another of the arts that Everett loved, and his parents hope that other mothers and fathers will establish similar living memorials to sons and daughters whose life songs break off after a stanza or two.

Everett Ruess Poetry Awards were offered to pupils of the Los Angeles High School in 1937–1938 and in 1938–1939. Poems and their writers receiving prizes or honorable mention in these contests included:

Tonight, Bonnie Barrett
Joy, Constance Peterson
To the Poetic Sense, Irving Juresco
The Wind, Georgyanna de Consigny
The City, Mildred Partridge
To Dr. Edwards, Sally Rubin
Horizons, Elna Sundquist
Dead Rainbow, Jane Mary Eklund
Testament, Stellita Paniagua
The Mirage, Millicent Rose Tag-von Stein
To a Pioneer, Marjorie Norton
Goodbye, Charlotte Quinn
To the Spain that Was, Floria Goldman
Sonnet, Patricia Geddes
Night Fantasy, Elizabeth Johnston
Merry-Go-Round, Beverly Morrison

These poems were printed in the Anthology of Student Verse, published by the Los Angeles High School, and edited by Snow Longley Housh, appearing in 1937, 1938 and 1939.[109]

Three Poems and Six Letters
by Everett Ruess

Previously Unpublished, from "Youth Is for Adventure"

Morning in Los Angeles Harbor

It is morning, and the ships again are stirring,
      Moving slowly from the harbor to the sea;
I can hear a distant tug boat's muffled purring,
      As it pulls a silent steamship on toward me.

It is morning, and the fog is slowly lifting
      From the misty docks and piers across the bay;
There is peace for me in barges slowly drifting
      And the silver stillness of awakening day.

—by Everett Ruess, 1929

The Air Circus

Diving, looping, rising, swooping,
Falling, curving, bracing, swerving,
      Turning in air—
Skidding, sliding, climbing, gliding,
Sprawling, slipping, zooming, dipping,
      All that they dare.
Softly moaning, loudly droning,
Higher leaping, upward sweeping,
      Wheeling around—
Racing, roaring, straining, soaring.
Rolling, spinning, lightly skimming
      Slowly to the ground.

—by Everett Ruess, 1929

The Ballad of the Lonely Skyscraper

Lonely you stand, among your lesser brothers;
You thrust your pointed way above them all,
Soaring into the sky with your tiered height
      And many-towered magnificence.

At dawn the sun lights up your eastern towers;
Men climb within your caverned corridors.
At noon your spires reach into scorching sun-
          glare.
Then you are dark against the sunset clouds,
And at your feet you cast long purple shadows.
Later you reach with grandeur to a starlit sky;
Men go, and leave you there to stand alone,
      Proud of your splendid stature.

You were not always here to pierce the clouds;
Once you were scattered in a thousand places.
From the firm earth men tore your ribs of
        steel.
Scarring the mountainsides with iron claws.
Gaunt, weatherbeaten oaks were felled
In far-off forests for your furnishings.
Huge blocks of granite once were carved and quarried
To make your pillared entrances.
Men gouged the wavelapped seashores
To make your concrete sides.
They tunneled deep beneath the earth
      To find a firm foundation for you.

Then, like a living thing you grew;
At each day's close you reached
A little nearer to the beckoning stars.
All day in your heights the riveters sweated,
Busily linking steel shafts with steel beams.
Higher and higher they toiled above the city;
Soon stone and wood and steel were made as
        one:
      At last you were completed.

Proudly you stand above your lesser brothers
        now,
Scorning the lowly dwarfs who made you
        great.
And I, who stand below in admiration,
        Worship your lofty loneliness.

      —Published in 1931 in "Builders and Makers"
      by Jean Lee Hunt, Harriet O'Shea, and others.

Point Lobos

Letter from Carmel, California, to Bill Jacobs, July 7, 1930

Point Lobos is really the one place I have seen which I prefer to all others. The cypresses are magnificent, and the ocean is a seething cauldron, whipping at the rocks. I found one place where there was a huge fissure in the rocks, making an island of one of them. Waves come in from each side. At one moment, you see the sun shining on the ocean. Then a huge wave comes, covering the opening and making it dark, like night. The force of the wave and the narrowness of the aperture forces the air and spray into your face, as if from a bellows. The whole rock shivers and trembles from the impact.

Wild Coastline

Program of the 1931 Artists and Adventurers' Expedition

A. & A. in chief: Lan Rameau (Eskeebi Killy)
      Official insignia: Green silk neckerchief
Mgr. Transportation of Supplies: Estimable Everett
      Official location notice (worn nightly): silver bell
      Official persuader: Pointed stick, 28 in. long (Never
        actually used. Employed only for ceremonial purposes)
      Official seal:
      Official indication of intense emotion: Switching of tail,
        followed by placing of official seal.
Dishwasher: Lau Ramean
Wood gatherer: Ran Lameau
Donkey driver: Nal Uaemer
Financier: Cherchez l'homme
Shoe-shiner: Lar Nameau
Cook: Fire does all the cooking
Door keeper: Behind schedule. Hasn't yet arrived. We all
      miss his services terribly.
Poet: Nar Lameau
Secretary: Aln Armeau
Treasurer: Superflous
Musical Entertainers: The Coyote Chorus
Retinue, Aides de Camp, etc: Such stray dogs, curious chipmunks,
      scavenging buzzards, and troubled tumblebugs as happen to
      follow after.
Official yell: 3 Brays, prolonged, and a Snort of Derision
Territory to be covered in 1931: The Great American Southwest

OFFICIAL SONG
      Whoopee, Kiyi, yo ho,
      Shake your feet, little burro,
      The faster you travel,
      The sooner you'll get there.
      Whoopee, Kiyi, yo ho,
      Shake your feet, little burro.

(In 1931 Everett for a time gave away his own name Everett to his burro and found himself a new, more euphonious name, Lan Rameau! Still later he took the name, Evert Rulan. Finally, his various names and pen-names causing confusion, he reverted to plain Everett Ruess.)

My Little Month-old Puppy, Curly

Letter from Kayenta, Arizona, to his Grandparents, May 1, 1931

Thanks for the crumbcake. It was hard, but I didn't give it to the donkey, you may be sure.

The picture of Grandpa, Father and me turned out very well, I thought.

A couple of days ago I helped a rancher butcher his calf and I am about to make a quirt from the hide.

My little, month-old puppy, Curly, has been a source of endless amusement, and with the foolish old burro, he keeps me well entertained. When the pup gets tired, I put him on the pack, and he rides with the burro. He likes to nip the donkey's heels, but he hasn't been kicked yet. His time will come.

Curly, taking a much-needed break.

I have just bought another canteen, a supply of food, and some oats for the burro. Tomorrow I shall be travelling again.

There was some heavy rain early this week, but now it is clear, and at night the full moon shines over the desert.

Now I must hurry and wash my clothes while the sun is high enough to dry them.

On the Crest of the Wave Again

Letter from San Francisco, California, to Mrs. Beatrice Whitnah, October 29, 1933

All's well, and I'm on the crest of the wave again, and hope you are too. I have finally found myself, and have been busy painting all day.

Yesterday I heard four symphonies, and then spent the afternoon and evening with Maynard Dixon, his wife Dorothea [Lange], Ernest Bacon, a musician, and some other artists. I had a grand time, and it was certainly good to be among friends and artists again.

I have a pleasant room. My kyaks and packs are in the corners, my pictures on the wall, and my Navajo blanket on the floor, so the room is truly mine. I overlook the street, and can see all that goes on . . .

I have done a little work at the aquarium already, and some at Telegraph Hill. To educate myself I heard Mischa Elman, saw Paul Robeson in "The Emperor Jones," and read with enjoyment the first volume of Lincoln Steffens' autobiography . . .

Best wishes to you and your family.

The Fiery Elixir of Beauty [110]

Letter from San Francisco, California, to his brother, Waldo, November 29, 1933

I have been fighting my way up tall hills between canyons of skyscrapers, hurling myself against the battling winds of Night, the raw swooping gusts that are like cold steel on my cheeks. I am drunk with a searing intoxication that liquor could never bring—drunk with the fiery elixir of beauty, the burning draught of power, and the soul piercing inevitability of music. Often I am tortured to think that what I so deeply feel must always remain, for the most, unshared, uncommunicated. But at least I have felt, have heard and seen and known, beauty that is inconceivable, that no words and no creative medium are able to convey. Knowing that the cards are stacked, and realized achievements, mere shadows of the dream, I still try to give some faint but tangible suggestion of what has burned without destroying me.

I was glad to find your letter, and I am happy that you are happy. I would believe in you even if you failed, but I do not think that you will. When events are over, it is often easier to trace the inevitability of their course. Have you not found it so? It is a genius, however, who can find in the past what will serve to plot the future. Most of us must wait until things have happened to see why they happened, and even then, we often do not see.

I Have Been Enjoying the City

Letter from San Francisco, California, to Mrs. Meinen, January 13, 1934

I was happy to find your letter last month, and glad to know that you are still your irrepressible self. Thanks too for buying the print. I have sold several since I've been here, and have raised the rate to three dollars for mounted prints. Some of them are showing at two galleries, and I have prospects of a third display.

The other day I made a journey through Chinatown with the sample of material you wanted and inquired at twenty or thirty shops, it seemed, but evidently styles pass even in China, and that design is out of print. I couldn't find anything that truly approximated it either, and I'm very sorry. At the Museum Wednesday I spent some while feasting my eyes on the fascinatingly beautiful Balinese designed in batik work. There is a whole room full of them.

I expect to make a sketching trip up the coast between here and Oregon in February. Shortly after, I'll be returning Hollywoodwards, and I'll be delighted to stop in and see you. But I might be dressed like an old tramp, so beware! After I get back home I shall have to lend most of my energies to ways and means of equipment for a year in Arizona. I mean to be there in April, and it ought to be a magnificent year.

I have been enjoying the city—revelling in books, music, new teritory and new friends. Sometimes I go for long walks of exploration in the rain and the wind.

You ought to see my beautiful coleus plant, with its symmetrically towering red and green leaves. It keeps changing shape all the time, as I turn it first one side out and then the other towards the light.

The sky is dark and lowering; the buildings are grey and pale. Storm ahead! The streets will be wet and gleaming, and lights will glitter in the rain.

Best wishes for jolly days in Santa Barbara.

Love from Everett

Tomales Bay, Fishing Shack

The Salt Lake Tribune's Account of Its 1935 Expedition to Southern Utah in Search of Everett Ruess

[from issues dated 24 August 1935, pp. 1, 10; 25 August 1935, p. 12; 26 August 1935, p. 10; and 27 August 1935, p. 10]

S. L. Tribune Expedition into Desert Finds Clues to Fate of Young Artist

Youth's Trail Retraced Over Wilderness and Reveals Evidence That He Probably Met Death at Renegade's Hands

Detailed story of The Salt Lake Tribune expedition, which made the search
for the missing artist, begins in the Monday edition.
It will be a graphic story of the west.

by John U. Terrell

Everett Ruess, 21-year-old missing Los Angeles artist, probably met death at the hands of a renegade bad man or Indian in a lonely canyon near the southern end of the untracked Escalante desert.

This is the united belief of the best Indian and white trackers, traders and wilderness residents of southern Utah and northern Arizona. Their conclusion is based on several "trails" of evidence, which to the men trained in the ways of remote lands, are almost irrefutable. But also these expressions of opinion have come following an extensive and intensive search by an expedition sent out by The Salt Lake Tribune, and which has practically exhausted other possibilities.

Trail Followed

Indian trailers employed by The Tribune expedition have established the fact that Ruess did not reach the Colorado river in his journey south from the town of Escalante, Utah, but probably met an untimely end in the little known Davis canyon, and his slayers carried off his valuable pack outfit—in all probability southward across both the Colorado and the San Juan rivers, into the fastnesses of the northern Navajo reservation.

As The Tribune expedition has reconstructed his disappearance: He left Escalante about November 12, 1934, traveling leisurely southward with his two burros. About 50 miles south of the town, he was seen by a sheepherder, the last person known to have seen him alive. In the course of some days, he covered the 100-odd miles across the barren sandy wastes, and reached the green pasture on the floor of Davis canyon.

There he made camp, turning his two burros into a small crudely fenced meadow near the upper end of the canyon. He hung a bridle and a halter on a fence post, built a campfire and prepared to remain a day or two. Probably within the next few days he climbed the great walls about him, and reached an ancient cliff dwelling, where he unearthed some pottery. He carried the several crumbling bowls and dishes down to his camp.

Find Last Campfire

Nearly four months later, a party of searchers from southern Utah followed Ruess' trail into Davis canyon. There they found the two burros still in the small pasture. Emaciated and weak, the two animals were spending their last strength in digging up roots to stave off complete starvation.[111] On the fence, where Ruess had placed them, were the bridle and the halter. Entering Davis canyon from the south, The Tribune expedition found the remains of Ruess' last campfire. The pottery was where he had placed it.

But still gone is the valuable trail outfit, and his grave remains undiscovered.

It was the first purpose of The Tribune expedition to discover if Ruess had himself gone on southward, possibly in the company of Indian friends, to the Navajo wilderness south of the two rivers. To reach the necessary starting point for such a search, the expedition worked northward from Navajo mountain in Arizona, and with the best Indian trailers available moved by pack train through the uninhabited canyon and mountain country, crossed both the Colorado and San Juan rivers and went on to Davis canyon. With the proved fact that Ruess had reached the point, the Indian trailers were set to work seeking a trail out of the canyon toward the only point where the Colorado river may be crossed.

Carried Valuables

Ruess carried in his outfit articles which would have attracted the eye of either a red or white outlaw, and especially renegade wilderness Indians, of which there are a number in the primitive Navajo country along the northern border of Arizona. He had a quantity of silver and turquoise jewelry, several fine Navajo blankets or rugs, a valuable camera, good outdoor clothing, a riding and a pack saddle, bright saddle blankets, $50 or $60 in cash, and perhaps holding less attraction were a bedroll of ordinary blankets, an expensive set of oil paints, a large black diary and notebook, a quantity of water colors, camp utensils and other articles of camp equipment.[112]

Previously, a paint brush found on the peninsula between the two rivers led to the belief he had gone that way. The Tribune expedition, trailing to the site where the brush was found, discovered there a number of ancient hieroglyphics and picture writings, which had been whitewashed for photographing. It was learned that the brush had belonged to a member of an archeological expedition who had photographed the cliff writings the previous year. Neither would the brush have been suitable for oil painting. And Ruess' parents, Mr. and Mrs. Christopher G. Ruess of Los Angeles, have denied that the brush belonged to their son, pointing out that it was a cheap type, for which he would have found no use in art work. All his art materials were of the most expensive make.

Old Tracks Remain

The person unfamiliar with the wilderness might logically presume that a trail seven months old could not be "picked up" by Indian trackers. The Tribune expedition received the word of Dougeye, famous Navajo trailer, that this was not the case, and it was he who led the way to places on the Colorado river trail where tracks of horses which had passed the previous December were clearly distinguishable. These places were close to great overhanging ledges of rock in narrow canyons where no rain ever strikes, and where the peculiar consistency of the soil preserves such marks ind[e]finitely. It was Dougeye's firm opinion that if a horse or a man on foot had crossed both rivers and entered the Navajo country on the only possible trail in this section, the tracks of the animal or the man's footprints would still exist and could easily be identified.

And although he proved this to the entire satisfaction of both Captain Neal Johnson and myself, we did not base our decision that Ruess had never crossed the rivers here on that fact alone.

Dougeye and other trailers produced evidence to show that only six persons—all Indians—had used the trail from the time Ruess made his last camp in Davis canyon until the ponies of The Tribune's expedition followed it—a period of eight months. All of these Indians have been identified. In November, 1934, Dougeye and two companions traveled northward over the trail to Escalante to trade for horses. In Escalante they saw Ruess and spoke with him. They left before Ruess began his journey, he following them out two days later.

Continue Search

When Dougeye, and his two partners, Hosteen Nath Godi and Azoli Begay, reached the rivers on the return trip, they met three other Indians traveling toward the north. And it was these six Navajos who passed over the narrow and dangerous trail during that period.

The Tribune expedition members did not stop at this seemingly unshakable conclusion that Ruess had gone no farther south. It was definitely learned, after many councils with Indians and traders, that even if all tracks of a person riding into the Navajo country from the north were obliterated, it would be impossible for that person to enter the country unseen, either by way of the Hole-in-the-Wall crossing, or at any other place.

And, standing firmly behind the assertion that had Ruess come into the Navajo country it would have been known at once, are Mr. Ray Dunn, the trader at Navajo mountain, nearest post to the river crossing; Mr. Buck Lowery of Marble Canyon, trader of many years' experience among northern Navajos; Mr. Carl Beck, Indian agent of Tuba City; Mr. John Wetherill, for forty years trader to the Indians and one of the best authorities on the country and its inhabitants; Mr. Ralph Jones, whose isolated trading post stands at Kaibeto Springs southwest of Navajo mountain; and numerous other white men and the most reliable and experienced Indians.

Traveled Alone

Ruess was a daring young man. He traveled alone in the wilderness, painting and writing as he went. But he was friendly and sociable, and wherever he went he made friends and acquaintances. All of the men mentioned knew him and had met him on previous trips he had made into the Navajo country. His plans were well known when he left Escalante, and in the last letter he wrote to his parents, dated November 11, 1934, he stated he was going southward to cross the rivers, and perhaps would be beyond civilization for two or three months.

Ruess' writings and letters reveal that he held a great love and appreciation for the wild, where he claimed he "dwelt with beauty and with peace." His attitude gave rise to the suspicion that he might have chosen to devote himself to a lonely and isolated life. The Tribune expedition considered this possibility at length and conducted an exhaustive investigation to determine if it was possible for a white youth to dwell any place within the Navajo country without it being known.

The invariable answer from Indian and white man was that such a thing was impossible. As to reasons, these were given: (a) A Navajo Indian cannot keep a secret. He reveals all such things to traders and agents. A white youth who had come to live among his people would be the choicest subject for gossip. The Indian would set out to learn why the white youth had come there to live; what were his intentions? why could he not dwell among his own people? (b) Had Ruess gone there to live, and to isolate himself from civilization, he would not have stopped painting and writing. Eventually his works would be seen, and most probably would have been pointed out by Indians, most of whom are deeply interested in all forms of art. (c) Ruess would have had to secure supplies, and no supplies are sold in the Navajo country except by licensed traders.

No Chance to Win

Ruess did not reach the Navajo country.

Did he leave his outfit in Davis canyon and strike out on foot? Dougeye smiled; the traders and trailers and agents laughed. No man could walk out of the desert country, across more than a hundred miles of burning wastes, where there are only a few springs, and these hidden in folds of the hills or under the ledges of deep canyons. And there are only those ways out which are watched by Indians, which lead directly to distant trading posts. Impossible. A stranger, equipped even with a good horse might perish on such a trip, if he was not fortunate in finding the little trickles of water which make any life possible in such a land.

And as the poker-faced Dougeye aptly put it: "White boy's outfit no have legs."

No, Ruess' outfit did not walk out of Davis canyon. He did not carry two heavy burro loads of equipment out on his back.[113] He did not leave his two burros, Chocolatero and Cockleburr[s], to starve to death in the little pasture in Davis canyon. Often he wrote stories of his burros, of his experiences with them, of his fondness and attachment for them, of the great length to which he had gone to train them and make them "good burros."

But with all this pointed out to it, the Tribune expedition continued on through the "beyond" of the Navajo country—to trading posts seldom visited by outsiders, to Indian camps, which lay at the end of the little used trails, to government agencies; held council after council, some of which lasted far into the night beside campfires, with Indians who were willing and eager to aid or to give any information they could.

And when civilization was reached again there remained only the unanimous conclusion—Everett Ruess, the young man whose eyes found beauty in the wilderness, whose heart found delight and peace there, made his last camp in Davis canyon one evening last November.

There the tricky and vicious hand of the renegade brought death to him—for the baubles and valuables he carried in his packs.

Here's History of Strange Disappearance at Outpost

by John U. Terrell

Everett Ruess, 21-year-old artist, whose home [is] in Los Angeles, wrote to his parents on November 11, 1934, from Escalante, Utah:

"I am going south toward the river now, through some rather wild country. I am not sure yet whether I will go across Smoky mountain to Lees Ferry, and south, or whether I will try and cross the river above San Juan. The water is very low this year. I might even come back through Boulder. So I may not have a postoffice for a couple of months. I am taking an ample supply of food with me."

Some days later he was seen by a sheepherder making his way to the Hole in the Rock on the Colorado river. It is at this point that the Navajos cross the river in their journeys north into Utah from the reservation.

Ruess got only as far as Davis canyon, a deep chasm feeding into the Escalante river approximately ten miles above the crossing of the Colorado. There he and his entire outfit, with the exception of two burros, a bridle and a halter, mysteriously vanished.

Everett Ruess' heart lay in the wilderness. Each year he spent his school vacation in the remote sections of the southwest. He was exceptionally well read, and himself wrote poetry, the theme of which invariably was the "wild." Wherever he went he carried with him his paints, and returned from his trips with many pictures, some of which revealed distinguished talent. Upon graduating from high school in Hollywood, he set out on an extended journey through the Navajo country and southern Utah. He was known at many isolated trading posts and Indian camps, to rangers and national parks officials. He had been wandering about northern Arizona and southern Utah for several months before he started on the trip across the great Escalante desert, from which he has never returned.

In the first part of last November he wrote to his brother, Waldo, a letter which clearly revealed his turn of mind in regard to life:

"As to when I shall visit civilization, it will not be soon, I think. I have not tired of the wilderness, rather I enjoy its beauty and the vagrant life I lead more keenly all the time. I prefer the saddle to the street car and the star-sprinkled sky to a roof, the obscure and difficult trail leading into the unknowns, to any paved highway, and the deep peace of the wild to the discontent bred by cities. Do you blame me, then, for staying here when I feel that I belong and am one with the world around me? It is true that I miss intelligent companionship, but there are so few with whom I can share the things that mean so much to me that I have learned to contain myself. It is enough that I am surrounded with beauty and carry it with me in things that are a constant delight, like my gorgeous Navajo saddle blankets, and the silver bracelet on my wrist, whose three turquoises gleam in the firelight . . . I know that I could not bear the routine and humdrum of the life you are forced to lead (in the city). I know I could never settle down. I have known too much of the deeps of life already, and I would prefer anything to an anticlimax."

His exceptional appreciation of wilderness things and the men and animals who live beyond the touch of civilization is vividly shown in a previous letter written to one of his friends in California. The letter, the true expression of a happy and enchanted youth, [can be found on pages 42–44].

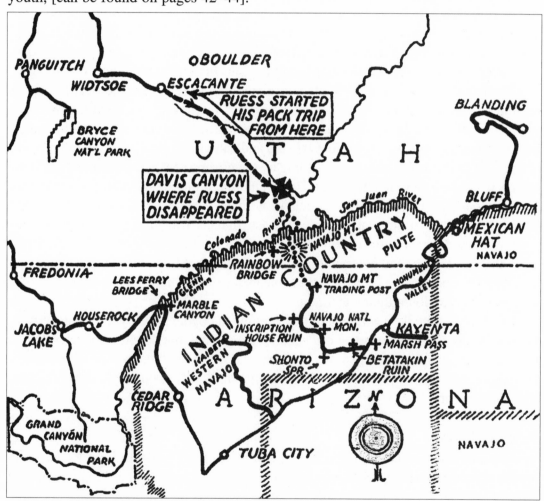

Route of the Salt Lake Tribune's *1935 Expedition in Search of Everett Ruess*

The map shows the route of The Tribune's expedition as it moved through the Navajo Indian country in northern Arizona and southern Utah. The heavy line starting at Blanding indicates the territory traversed by the expedition's automobile. From the Navajo Mountain Trading Post a pack train worked its way (shown by the dotted line) northward across both the San Juan and the Colorado rivers to Davis canyon, where Everett Ruess was known to have made his last camp. It was in Davis canyon that his burros were found. The dash line running from Escalante, Utah, southward to Davis canyon is the trail Ruess followed before he vanished. The major part of the territory shown is without roads of any grade, and is crossed by only a few narrow horse trails.

Navajos Gave Help in Hunt for Artist

Detailed Story Begins of Tribune Expedition in Search for Lost L.A. Painter

by John U. Terrell

This is the detailed story of The Salt Lake Tribune expedition's search, just completed, for Everett Ruess, missing young Los Angeles artist, who, in November, 1934, made his last camp in remote Davis canyon, near the San Juan river, ten miles above the place that stream feeds into the turbulent Colorado.

We were 17 miles west of Blanding, Utah, and there, in Allen canyon, at the trading store of Joe Hatch, we began our unceasing questioning, which was to continue without abatement for days and nights to come, as we worked farther into the uninhabited and little known territory which spreads in vast canyons, deserts and mountains over several hundred miles bordering the San Juan and Colorado rivers.

On this evening we sat with Hatch before his small store high in the Bear Ears hills, surrounded by the moonlit La Sal forest. Between the trading post and the San Juan river to the south was a rough country of deep washes, sheer canyons and wind-swept peaks, inhabited only by a few Piute Indians and cattlemen. Nearly all the Indian men, about 130, were employed at trail building by the government. They were then camped not far from the store. This had given Hatch an opportunity to question them about the missing youth. He had held several councils with head men when they had come to the post for supplies, to no avail. Many of these Indians had, during the previous six months, hunted horses in the country bordering the San Juan on the north. We had their word that no stranger had entered this section during that time, and, inasmuch as several white cowboys also had ridden the same territory and made the same report, there was no reason to doubt their statements.

About us as we talked with Hatch that evening, a coyote pup, a young dog and two kittens romped. When we spread out beds on the ground, the coyote at once curled on the corner of a blanket and spent the night there. Occasionally he would whimper and crawl close to one of the men, nosing about until the sleeper had wakened and scratched its ears.

Rode Burro

With the fact in mind that Everett Ruess was seen heading south from Escalante in the middle of November, 1934, it was our immediate purpose to ascertain if he had crossed the San Juan and Colorado rivers and entered the Navajo country. Leaving Escalante, Ruess' outfit consisted of two burros, Chocolatero and Cockleburr[s], one of which he rode. The other he used to transport his camp outfit, his oil paints, valuables consisting of silver and turquoise jewelry, Navajo blankets and money, oil paints and canvases and clothing.

At Davis canyon, the two burros, nearly dead from starvation, had been found in a small pasture, which they had cropped clean. Neither Ruess nor any part of his personal or camp outfit has ever been found.

As to whether he had ever traveled himself beyond Davis canyon, only the Navajos could tell. Only they, and comparatively few of them, ever cross the Colorado river. They sometimes come up into the southern Utah country in the late fall to trade for horses in the vicinity of Escalante. We had every assurance that this paramount question could be solved, if we were able to find certain Indians known to have made trading trips north into Utah late last year.

The country into which Everett Ruess may have wandered, if he crossed the two rivers, lies roughly between the post at Mexican Hat and Lees Ferry. It is approximately 300 miles in length from east to west and 100 miles in width from north to south. But one cannot traverse it on a straight road. One must follow torturous trails, mere wagon tracks winding through rocky washes, clinging to the sides of precipices, climbing over mountains and mesas. Only part of it can be crossed in a car or wagon; in most of it, one must depend upon a Navajo pony or the faithful burro. There are no trading posts and no permanent Indian camps north of Navajo mountain, which rises to a heighth of more than 10,000 feet near the center of the northern half of the territory. Thus, between the mountain and the two rivers is the most primitive country, without habitation or definable trail, seldom seen by white men, and traversed only spasmodically by small bands of nomadic Navajos.

We had, however, an important factor in our favor. Because the country was so completely wild, a stranger, and especially a white youth, would have been seen had he passed through it.

"You may go through it without seeing an Indian," an old trader told us, "but don't ever think the Indians won't see you. It would be impossible to ride through that country and not be seen."

We received this same word from others—traders, stockmen, government agents and Indians. It is a poor country in which to attempt to hide. And we were told of criminals who had escaped into it, believing themselves safe, only to be quickly apprehended by deputies led by Indians.

Tracks Trailed

"The Indians can tell even when a strange horse goes through the country," a government agent said. "And if they see tracks they immediately investigate. If they don't see anyone, they go to the nearest post or agency and say: 'White man in the country. Why?' Only one criminal I know of in 20 years ever passed through without being caught. He turned the shoes around on his horse and rode at night. The Indians were puzzled. 'Horse all come, no go,' they said. But we got the man later."

We felt encouraged by this information. If Everett Ruess had come to harm south of the Colorado or San Juan rivers, or if he had entered the country, even though he had passed directly through it, it was probable that we would learn of it.

Returning to Blanding from the Bear's Ears, we went southwestward through Bluff and Mexican Hat. The telephone line ends at Bluff, and when we left it behind we had no way of communicating with civilization. Between Bluff and Kayenta, more than 100 miles south, there is no mail route. The road, only two ruts wandering through deep valleys and across high sage covered mesas, seems uncertain of its destination. In the afternoon we came to Monument valley, ascended the pass of the same name, from which we could see an endless confusion of red mountains and barren desert, and moved into a country whose chief characteristic was gigantic red and yellow walls rising sheer for several hundred feet about us. We reached Kayenta at sundown.

There were two Indians we especially wanted to see at Kayenta. But first we held a long conference with John Wetherill, who for more than 40 years has been a trader to the Navajos.

"Dead," John Wetherill said with quiet firmness. He outlined his reasons for drawing such a conclusion, and they were convincing. "But," he added, "you want specific evidence. Well, if there was a white boy living among the Navajos for any reason on earth, I would have heard of him."

Here again we were told that a Navajo Indian cannot keep a secret. Here again we were told that no white man could enter or pass through the Navajo country without being seen, and in all probability identified.

"If Everett Ruess crossed the Colorado and entered country adjoining, what would he be living on all this time? (Nearly seven months had passed since Everett was thought to have crossed the river and ridden south.) He'd have to come out for supplies," John Wetherill continued. "And there are no Indians living along either river in the winter time."

We were favored by a moon in our night journey, and when we left the post at Kayenta it was topping the pinons on the high eastern mesa. Our guide drove us several miles out into the desert and when leaving the car we set out on foot, crossed an Indian cornfield planted where water seeps from beneath the cliffs, and struck out through sage and cactus. The camp we wanted, our guide told us, was on a rugged rise which we could make out ahead against the bright light of the sky.

Seeking Advice

I have forgotten the Indian's name. It was, for me, unpronounceable. He was, however, Natani, which means "wise man" or sometimes "head man." The Navajos have no chiefs. They have only these elders of the clan, whom they respect and revere. They are ordinarily advanced in years, gray and wrinkled, and it is conceded that long life has given them wisdom and the ability to lead.

It was Natani, and Natani's wife, with whom we wished to hold council. Natani is a medicine man; his wife is renowned as a seer. But it was not that we wished Natani to call upon the Indian gods to aid us, rather we wanted practical advice and any information he may have had. However, I had no notion in mind to ignore any message Natani or his wife might ring down from the Navajo spirits. My experience with medicine men had been too wide for that. And what we were told in the way of information that had come through the charm of the "great medicine" rather astounded us.

We found Natani's camp, consisting of two brush hogans. Round about the desert, washed in the yellow moonlight, reached away to the dim shadowy walls of the high mesas. Several shaggy dogs growled as we came up and retreated to the safety of a hogan. Three men and a woman were grouped near a doorway. Natani and his wife had retired. During our entire visit they remained partly wrapped in their blankets thrown carelessly on the ground. Natani's wife was perhaps 20 years younger than he. I learned later that she was his third wife; two others, nearer his own age, also lived in the camp. But this younger woman held spiritual powers that few women of the tribe possessed; we might, in our way, speak of her as "psychic"; it was "strong medicine" to the Indians. She brought added influence and "power" to Natani.

Talk of New Deal

We smoked, not in this case a pipe of peace, but cigarets bought at an extremely high price in the trading post. They served equally as well. And for an hour we talked of a great variety of things, of horses and men, or rain and heat, of "Washingdon" of whom the Indians have learned much since the new deal was launched. Government money and government men have flowed together into the reservation; the Indians have been employed to build roads, reservoirs, to erect windmills, to conserve water and forests, and they are being taught the danger of overgrazing and soil erosion. Natani seemed to enjoy speaking of all this new knowledge "Washingdon" had brought to him. He made a speech on erosion, and I began to fear the night would not be long enough to hold it. In part, as interpreted to us by our guide, it ran:

"Washingdon says we can have more water if we learn his ways of saving it. Washingdon says it is water that ruins the grass for our sheep. The water carries away the earth and the grass cannot grow. This is because our sheep have eaten too much and the grass will not hold the earth when the rain sweeps down upon it. Washingdon is wise this way. But if we have not our sheep, what will we do? No, Washingdon says, keep your sheep and we will make the grass grow and save the earth. We will build dams to hold back the water. We will send the sheep to eat at one place today and tomorrow they will eat another place. We will put our shoulders against the arroyas and hold back the earth that would disappear. Washingdon says the sheep and the wagon wheels have made the arroyas. The sheep walk on a trail, beating down the earth. Then the rain comes and the water runs down the same trail over the bare earth. Soon the earth sinks and the arroya is begun. Washingdon says the wagon wheels have done this too. Natani can look back to his youth and remember the country when there were no arroyas and the grass stood against his stomach where he walked. Washingdon says the tall grass will return if we obey."

Our guide explained that we were old friends of his seeking one lost six months before, and Natani's shining black eyes were fastened on us.

Wife Speaks

"Why have you waited so long to look for your friend?" he inquired quite logically, but he appeared satisfied with the explanation that we had not known Everett Ruess was lost until three months before.

Here for the first time Natani's wife spoke. "Far north," she said almost inaudibly.

The guide nodded, and added, "But he may have come this way. We wish to know if he lives or if he has gone away and remains only in our memories. We wish to know if he has made his last camp. Where did he make it? Why has he not come back to speak to us?"

We remained silent. The Indians at the hogan moved to sit about us. A heavy bank of clouds was rising in the north. I felt a drop of rain strike me. But the south country was still flooded with brilliant moonlight. Behind me a squaw spoke. We turned our heads. In the hogan a dog growled.

A figure was moving toward us, cut against the bright light. It was a tall, young Indian cowboy. He sat down in the outer circle.

The guide spoke to us. "We'll get down to business now. There's no hurrying this. If you haven't seen this before, try not to laugh, no matter what she does. She sometimes gets pretty emotional. But before we are through, we'll know something. If anybody in this whole country can help you, they can. If any Indian knows anything about this, they do. But he won't tell you anything as if it came from his own mind. It's got to come out of the medicine and the gods. Even if he knew a good deal, he'd have to get it from the medicine before he'd tell you."

Indians Furnish Clue to Lost Artist's Trail

Medicine Man's Wife Draws Directions on Sand for Searchers to Follow

by John U. Terrell

Natani had opened his shirt and drawn out a medicine bag. His wife had covered her face. Almost at the moment he began to chant softly the rain fell. Great large drops pattered on the sand and sagebrush. We sat huddled over, but in a few minutes our backs were soaked. There was no stopping now. No one moved. The chant grew louder, but never rising above the singsong rhythmic way the Navajo medicine man calls upon his gods. Natani's wife weaved slowly back and forth. She lifted her shoulders. Dipping into the sacred little buckskin bag, Natani drew out a pinch of medicine dust and sprinkled it over his wife, not for an instant hesitating in his "sing."

Wife Makes Signs

She suddenly uncovered her face, bent forward and let her fingers run through the sand. Twice she threw the "earth" over her bosom. In the sand she built a mound; she indicated crooked lines running from it. I knew then that she was building Navajo mountain, the sacred mountain that rises approximately 150 miles north and west of Kayenta, and I tried to recall all I had heard of this Indian shrine. On its timbered top certain gods come down to the earth. On it various spirits dwell. It is hallowed ground, no place for mortal Indian, and no Navajo ever remains on it after sundown. All day he may hunt horses on its great rough slopes, or hunt, but always he starts down as the sun falls. At darkness the mountain is left to the gods.

Natani's wife twice destroyed the miniature mountain her quick hands built. It was not right, or perhaps she had erred in following her spiritual instructions. Patiently she built it a third time, never raising her eyes to look on other faces. Natani sang, moving his thin shoulders slightly with the rhythm of his song, his voice fine and resonant, beauty in every tone. The rain grew colder, fell harder.

Now the mountain was finished, the crooked lines running from it (the deep canyons) apparently were drawn satisfactorily. To the north of the mountain Natani's wife drew a long line twisting and running generally southwest. From this line a finger trailed almost directly east, leaving a smaller, though no less twisted, line. The converging point of these two lines was almost directly north of the sacred mountain, perhaps in the scale of her map a distance of 30 miles. They were the Colorado and San Juan rivers.

Scene Ends Abruptly

The chant ended abruptly. Natani's wife sat with head fallen, breathing deeply, as if she were very tired. The rain stopped, the cloud bank breaking and drifting across the brilliant sky in small fragments.

Natani spoke: "Go to the forks of the rivers."

Guide: "He lives there?"

Natani: "He was there. Close by he made a camp. You will find the fire."

Guide: "Have you seen him?" (He meant in a vision.)

Natani: "He has gone away from there."

Guide: "He's dead."

Natani: "He has gone away and does not mean to come back."

Guide: "He went away without his camp outfit?"

Natani: "I do not see that clearly. There is a shadow. Only some of his outfit was moved away. There is more some place. I see him talking with two friends. They are Navajos. Young men like himself. They sing and eat together. Then there is a shadow. He has gone away. The Navajos have left the place. They are no longer with him. She says they have traveled together. He (Ruess) has given himself to our gods. He has taken us in his arms and wished to come among us."

Guide: "Does she say he came into the Navajo country?"

Natani: "She says he did not. He went away there where he camped."

Say Follow Advice

During the next two days we talked with white traders, with government men of long experience among the Indians, with white guides and stockmen who not only speak the Navajo tongue, but understand the Indian customs and characters. Invariably, upon hearing Natani's message, they gave one answer: "Do as he told you."

"You can take it lightly if you want to," one old trader said, "and I wouldn't say I believed in Indian medicine, either. But I learned long ago never to laugh at it. I've seen too many strange things happen. Those fellows are uncanny, and if I were you I'd head straight for the forks of the rivers."

It was a government agent of long experience, however, who seemed to see the situation in a more practical light. He said: "I'd bet my last dollar that Everett Ruess was near the Colorado if Natani said he was. With good Indian trackers you can probably pick up some sort of trail. But if Natani told you he didn't come into the Navajo country from the north, you bet he didn't."

"We know Ruess camped in Davis canyon," I said.

"Sure," was the reply, "and Natani told you the same. If there's a trail, it will be there. But if Natani said you won't find Ruess there, you can just forget about it."

Start for Mountain

Nevertheless, we didn't forget about it. But when the sun came up we were on the way to Navajo mountain. Even a poor map will give an idea of the primitiveness of the country ahead of us. We followed a wagon road toward March pass and, after this point, turned off on a trail that seemed unconcerned with hills, cliff faces or deep washes. In places we put the battered car over great flat reaches of gray rock on which no tracks showed. One of us went ahead to find the place where tracks left the rocks. Several times we plunged foot by foot up steep slopes keeping the wheels blocked with rocks. Then suddenly we would emerge into a beautiful forest of scrub pine and cedar through which the winding trail would be as smooth as a city street. These places were few and small, however.

In the early afternoon we descended a tortuous dugway across the face of a great cliff. Far below were a series of deep gorges and chasms. And halfway down this trail, which was scarcely wide enough in places for us to keep all wheels on solid earth, we met an Indian with a wagon drawn by two perspiring mules. For a time we sat and stared at the Indian; he at us. But at last we all laughed. We got out, and managed somehow to work out a plan. Although we neither could understand the language of the other, it was decided that the wagon, being the lighter of the two vehicles, would have to be moved to the top of some rocks along the dugway. We, with the amazing strength of the little mules, got the front of the wagon on the rocks. The car was moved forward against the rear wheels of the wagon, and its front wheels were then lowered back into the roadway. The rear end was hoisted onto the rocks, and the car moved into clear space. We sat down then with the Indian and silently smoked a cigaret. Occasionally, he would glance at us and laugh. This was the sum total of our conversation, but it was pleasant enough.

Find Trading Post

At the foot of the narrow trail, in a canyon of awe-inspiring depth, were the springs of Betatakin. Here was a trading post and a small lodge of hogans for travelers through the Indian country. We secured directions, ate a lunch, bought a few gallons of gas which the trader syphoned from a barrel with a rubber hose, and started on. The Navajo mountain road ascended a great hill of bright yellow sand on which some crushed stone had been scattered. Without the stone and the latticed sand fences which prevented drifting, an ascent would have been impossible. From the top of the hill the road turned sharply toward the north, and now, looking back into the canyon of the great yellow walls, the trading post and the cabins appeared like several small boxes thrown away beside the bright green cottonwoods growing about the spring.

During the rest of the afternoon we occasionally sighted an Indian rider, now and then we saw a small band of wild horses which disappeared from view with heads up and tails flying. We passed no habitation, but it was understood that lost somewhere in the folds of the rough hills were Indian camps. Perhaps Indian eyes could have found them. The country became rougher as we went northward, and at last the hills vanished and we followed the thread of trail through an intricate network of canyons, creeping along beneath towering brilliantly colored walls. We saw no water, except that caught in the pockets of the flat rocks. It is from these rainwater pools in the rocks that both Indians and stock get water part of the year. Without them it would be impossible to exist in this section.

See Mountain Ahead

Always ahead, towering above the world, now stood Navajo mountain, its blue timbered slopes appearing cool and inviting. Rain swept over the crest like great blue brooms, and as we at last climbed out of the canyon country onto the wooded uplands, the rain reached us, and the mountain was lost in thick clouds. With each mile the trees grew larger, and when we had reached an altitude at which rain falls intermittently throughout the year we entered a forest over which great yellow pines predominated, holding shaggy heads above the gnarled cedars and lesser trees. The sun had fallen behind the mountain when we descended into a heavily wooded canyon through which spring water seeped, and stopped before Dunn's Navajo mountain trading post.

This was the end of the wagon road. Between the post and the two rivers, a distance of twenty-five miles, lay only an uncharted region known to only a few Indians and fewer white men. It was a land without trails, without camps, with a few hidden water holes. And it was across those rivers, in a small box canyon where there was pasturage and water that Everett Reuss' two burros had been found several months before. It was somewhere along those rivers that he had, according to Natani, "gone away."

We employed an interpreter, and through him learned that no Indians had crossed the Colorado river since late the previous fall. Then an old man, half Piute, half Navajo, stepped forward from the group in the post. He had seen Reuss last November in Escalante. He remembered him well, remembered his outfit. The old Indian, bow-legged, gaunt, with shining black eyes and long coarse hair falling from under his great hat, was named Dougeye.

"He's the best tracker in here," Mr. Dunn said. "And he knows that country better than anybody else."

We told him our story. We explained our mission. And at last we told him what Natani had said. Would he take us there? The price had to be settled first. He considered the proposition, purchased a chocolate bar, carefully folded the tinfoil which had been about the bar and stowed it in a pocket, munched on the candy. He turned to the interpreter, moved a hand in an arc above the earth and spoke.

"He means at the second sun he'll take you," the interpreter said. "Tomorrow he has to get his horses. Then the next morning at dawn he'll come for you. He says it will take three pack horses, because grass is poor and his horses are not strong."

"Can we depend on him?" I inquired.

Mr. Dunn answered promptly. "I've traded with him a long time, and I'd say he'll be here if the sun comes up that morning."

About a campfire that night we made our plans. There were a dozen places to be visited yet; there were more Indians in distant parts of the reservation to talk with; there were other sections to be searched.

Discuss Our Plans

We spent the following day talking through our interpreter with numerous Indians who drifted into the post. It was amazing how swiftly the news of our arrival traveled. Squaws came dragging little children to look at us. They stood outside the post peering at us. Often the doorway was filled with heads. When we went out they quickly dropped their eyes and moved away; but from vantage points they kept black eyes filled with curiosity fastened on us.

Dougeye was as good as his word. He arrived at dawn with the horses. We were assigned to ponies so small that it seemed almost a certainty they could not carry us. How badly mistaken was this thought. At the end of the first day on the trail I felt convinced these ponies were close ancestors to the feline species. They would hop up on boulders, nimbly drop off again. They went sure footedly along perilous ledges, seeming totally unaware that death waited in the yawning chasms below. They nibbled at succulent blades of grass as they struggled on a three-foot trail up the face of a cliff.

It was magnificent country; in part, thick forest, elsewhere bare red rock, sweeps of green pinon, vast reaches of sage. The sacred mountain crossed, we looked upon a world resembling an endless tossing red and yellow sea, still turbulent after being stirred to its depths by a great storm. During the long afternoon the trails led continuously downward, and at night we were camped beside the San Juan.

Recent rains had raised it to a dangerous level. Dougeye stood staring at it, and at last shook his head. "No cross."

We told him we had to cross. And in the morning, stripping his outfit down to bare necessities, Johnson plunged in. It was a wild scramble. Twice one of the pack horses, a little roan which seemed unused to such swift water, went under. The roan came up each time coughing and only fighting the harder to master the current. We were wet, chilled, but eagerly we went on. We were on the peninsula now where, ill-founded rumor had it, Everett Reuss had made a camp.

Desert Folk Believe Ruess Killer Victim

Medicine Man's Wife Draws Directions on Navajos Who Took Expedition Over Wild

by John U. Terrell

(The Tribune expedition sent out to search for the missing California artist, Everett Ruess, who disappeared in the wild and remote country bordering the Colorado and San Juan rivers, has reached by pack trails the peninsula between those two turbulent streams and are nearing the canyon in which Ruess is known to have made his last camp before he and his entire pack outfit mysteriously disappeared. This is the last installment.)

Several hours later, Dougeye shook his head again in his characteristic way. We had crossed the peninsula and there was no campsite on the trail, no old ashes, and, most important of all, no burro tracks or footprints. "White boy not camp here," Dougeye said.

Although the Colorado was "fast water," crossing it proved easier. Wet again, we pushed steadily up the trail toward Davis canyon. Dusk caught us and Dougeye proved his worth again. Turning sharply, he led us into a small side canyon. There, hidden beneath a great ledge of yellow rock, was a small, clear spring of cold water.

It was at daylight that we came to the place where the paint brush was found. A few yards away, on the wind-worn surface of a cliff, we found the tell-tale hieroglyphics. They had been whitewashed for photographing. Dougeye knew when the archeologist had visited the place.

"Gravehunter," Dougeye called him. "Get lost, too. We find three days. Not lost. Crazy."

Overstayed Time

We understood that the man had merely overstayed his time in the country, and, in the opinion of the simple Dougeye, had little to do indeed if he spent his time crawling around picture writings and cliff ruins.

We both felt that in this discovery we had made certain that Ruess had not reached the Colorado. And we went on to Davis canyon. Dougeye led us to Ruess' campsite. There were the remains of a fire. There were burro tracks. We thought longingly of the camera which we had been unable to carry because of Dougeye's fear of such contraptions. He refused to have anything to do with the search if it went along. I was consoled with the thought that in all probability it would have been ruined in crossing the rivers. And I dared not arouse Dougeye's superstitions. He had objected in the beginning to searching for a dead man, for fear he would find him. When it had been mentioned in the post that Ruess may be dead, several Indians at once departed and were not seen again. The Navajo will have nothing to do with the dead, even refusing ordinarily to hunt for a body.

No Raft Built

We set Dougeye to working on the trail out of Davis canyon. His final verdict was: "White boy come in, not go out."

"You mean he didn't walk or ride out?" I asked.

Dougeye stared at me, fear plain in his obsidian eyes. I understood what he meant.

Then Ruess was buried somewhere here, we concluded. But Dougeye shook his head. "No grave. Could find."

I inquired if it was possible that Ruess could have gone down the river on a raft . . . to his death.

"Raft and packs would float," was Dougeye's quiet reply, and we saw the wisdom in this conclusion. The river is closely watched at such places as Lees Ferry. Then

Dougeye added a final blow to this speculation, abruptly halting it.

"Only few places where raft could be made. Me went there look. No raft made."

Continued Search

It was nearly ten miles from the Davis canyon trail to the Colorado river. It was inconceivable that Ruess would pack his outfit to the river and return to place his burros in the canyon. There were better canyon pastures at the crossing of the river.

For two days we continued to search Davis canyon and the country running down to the river. We could not shake Dougeye's conviction; we found no track, except those made by the horses of the Indians previously mentioned who had passed through the country. That was all. We started on the hard journey back to the Navajo Mountain post, nearly 30 miles away.

Johnson wanted to search several other places en route, just to "leave no stone unturned." I pushed on, after we had agreed to meet at Marble canyon, 200 miles by trail to the southwest.

Early in the morning I turned the car, badly bent and beaten but apparently with all its old-time tenacity and will intact, back over the trail from the post, with Kaibeto my destination.

Knew Country Well

Kaibeto, had I been able to travel with the crows, was only 35 miles across the country from the Navajo Mountain post. It was more than 100 by the trail I was obliged to follow. But my journey to Kaibeto was abruptly halted when I had got back to Betatakin. There I was advised by a government man that it would be prudent to get the names of certain Indians in the Kaibeto district before visiting there. And the man who could supply me with those names, Buck Lowry, was at Lees Ferry, nearly 200 miles away. I reached Tuba City, after crossing the northwest corner of the Hopi country, that evening, and after getting supper at the post I went on to the Gap. The remaining 65 miles to Lowry's lodge at Marble canyon I covered early the next morning.

Before I started back toward Kaibeto I had obtained the names of three Indians whom I was assured I could depend on for information and assistance. They were Hosteen Geishi; his son, Geishi Betah, and a kinsman, Roy Nez. But I had also obtained a clear picture of the situation confronting me as it was drawn by Mr. Lowry, who had for many years been a trader at Kaibeto and who understood well the way of the country and its people.

Hopeless Feeling

This was the picture:

Presuming Everett Ruess had reached the Colorado or the San Juan, when his supplies gave out, he would be obliged either to travel southward until he reached a trading post in the Navajo country, or turn back to Escalante, 100 miles to the north across an empty, burning desert. He might have obtained some supplies from the few sheep or cattle men who live in the country bordering the rivers a part of the year. But if this had been done it would have been reported. Not a man lives in southern Utah or northern Arizona who does not know much of the details of the long search.

Perhaps Everett attempted to trail down the north side of the Colorado to the nearest settlement in this direction, Lees Ferry, 100 miles from the forks. But there is no established trail through this country; the few waterholes are hidden and could only be found by one knowing well the country; and there are no inhabitants. And he could not have moved without burros.

All this, it may be understood, was speculation. I was trying to find a loophole in the evidence we had that Ruess had never left Davis canyon; I was trying to break down Natani's story; and all the time I held the feeling that it was hopeless.

"Hosteen Geishi can tell you," Mr. Lowry said. "If Ruess entered the country north of Kaibeto, he or some of his men will know it. A strange horse track will start them investigating, and you can be certain that if they say Ruess did not enter the country south of the river, he didn't."

At Tuba the next evening, on my way to Kaibeto, I thought of what I had learned of Hosteen Geishi. He was very old. When he was a youth he had fallen and broken his leg. For a long time he walked with a crutch. This story is told in the word geishi, which in the Navajo tongue signifies crutch. The name remained, was handed down from father to son and to grandson.

Years ago Hosteen Geishi discovered a gold lode on Navajo mountain. It was a fabulously rich lode, but the Indians did nothing toward development. Seldom they took out any ore. Eventually, however, two educated Indians carried some samples to the outside world. They proved exceptionally high grade. Three miners returned with the Indians. But before they ever reached the mine, the three white men and the two Indians were shot to death.

It was the geishi way of saving their country from a gold rush. And today old Hosteen Geishi retains the secret of his gold mine. A number of other white men and Indians have sought to learn its whereabouts, but Hosteen Geishi remains silent. Often some of the Indians of the district have agreed to lead parties to the mine, but always they led them some other place and laughingly collected for guiding service.

'Want No Gold'

"We want no gold," Hosteen has said. "We are well off with sheep and cattle and horses. We have many children and live happily in our country. The white men would ruin all this for us. I have forgotten where the gold is."

It wasn't gold I wanted of Hosteen Geishi. It was word of a piece of the camp outfit of Everett Ruess. It was to look at the dead black ashes of an old campfire. It was word of his bones, which I felt convinced lay safe in a hidden place in the vast wilderness. But when I reached Kaibeto, bearing a letter from Carl Beck, the Indian agent at Tuba, and the names of the Indians Mr. Lowry had given me, I was told by Mr. Jones, the trader, that Hosteen Geishi was very ill, standing at the gate to the happy hunting ground.

"And the secret of the gold mine will go with him?" I asked.

"Probably some of the others know where it is," Mr. Jones answered. "But it's just as safe with them as it was with old Hosteen. These men have grown up with that secret. Holding it has become a tradition. But Geishi Betah is here, and he knows more about the river country than anybody else."

Interpreter Used

There was a chicken and rabbit dinner to be eaten first. Afterward I called my interpreter. In front of the post we sat down. Before me in the sand I drew a crude map of the river country. A dozen Indians joined the circle. They were handsome, willowy fellows in high-heeled boots and immense hats. They wore their hair in a braided knot at the back. It was sleek and as black as the pitchrock of the canyons. Turquoise ornaments dripping from their ears; silver bracelets, strings of coral and turquoise about their necks. I wondered how old that coral was . . . hundreds of years. It was never found in the southwest, but was brought by the early Spaniards from the Indies. The Navajos have had it ever since.

These were the riders of the wilderness, and Geishi Betah, a fine old Indian with a sculptured bronze face and a bright yellow headband, was their leader. What Geishi Betah told me that day left little doubt in my mind that Everett Ruess ever had entered the Navajo country from the north.

As I got it through the interpreter, Geishi Betah felt certain that he or some of his men would have crossed a strange trail. His men hunted horses on the San Juan river late last fall. Then came heavy snows. No man could have survived the winter in such a country without coming out for supplies. And it was known that Everett had no more than two months' supplies when he headed south from Escalante on November 12.

Few Camping Spots

"Go north of the Colorado," Geishi Betah said. "There are many places there a man might die, but only one, two, three, four, five (he counted them on crooked fingers) where a man might camp. Man camps only at water."

My interpreter suggested that Everett might have been killed by renegade Indians who wanted his outfit. Geishi Betah's eyes searched my face.

"You do not believe that," he said.

"I have nothing to believe yet," I answered.

He talked softly.

"I know every Indian in that country, every one who passed through. We have seen them and we know their business."

The interpreter chanced an uncomplimentary remark.

"Washington will send a policeman to look at all the outfits of the Indians and talk with them."

I thought a slight smile touched Geishi Betah's lips. He stared for a moment at the young interpreter who had learned so well in Washington's school to sling the words of two tongues about.

Proffers Help

"We will help the policeman," was the quiet answer. "The white boy did not come south of the river, and his outfit did not walk here alone. I think he has gone away from us. Send the policeman, tell Washington. We want no trouble."

It was dark when my interpreter and I reached Tuba.

I held several councils there, another at the Gap, another at Marble canyon. Day after day I talked with trailers, hunters, trackers, cowboys, sheepherders, medicine men. In traveling about the reservation I crossed my own trails until I became known. And one day near Tuba I met an Indian I could not recall having spoken to. He waved at me as I was driving across a burning desert flat.

"Yahte'h (hello) Man-Looking-for-Boy," he said. "No find?"

"No find," I said.

"Dead long ago," he said. "Goodbye. Thanks."

News Travels Fast

News travels swiftly over the barren wastes and high ranges of the Navajo country. I doubt if a newspaper would bring the day's events to the most isolated inhabitants any faster. It was known, for instance, that I carried a camera, and at last I was obliged to keep it hidden in the car. Arriving at a camp, eyes swiftly searched for it. There was

no council until I had given assurance I wished to make no pictures. And not even presents of bright jewelry or perfume would make welcome the "box with winking eye." They wanted none of it.

Day after day, and often into the night, I continued to ask my questions, and when Johnson reached Marble canyon, we held a last council. We put all our "medicine" in the circle. The Indians, the traders, the guides, the interpreters, the cowboys and shepherds and prospectors spoke again, for the last time.

This is the result: Everett Ruess was murdered in the vicinity of Davis canyon. His valuable outfit was stolen. He never reached the Colorado river.

"But some day," we said, "pieces of his outfit will turn up."

Then we would take the trail again.

"There are . . . only [a few places] . . . where a man might camp. Man camps only at water."

"In Search of an Old Inscription: Utah Trip 1935"
by Stella Knight Ruess

Because our young artist son Everett had mysteriously vanished in southern Utah in the winter of 1934–5, my husband Christopher and I decided to spend our vacation there in June [1935]. We had had much correspondence with the kind people who had searched for Everett, and had shown a deep interest in his personality and his fate. In November 1934, he had sent us twenty of his watercolors and a ten dollar gift, which we immediately spent in having several of these framed. They have been a joy to us on our living room walls ever since. A collection of his paintings has been exhibited on several occasions.

We did not expect to find [any] trace of Everett, when so many others had failed, but it gave us great satisfaction to meet these good friends who were so interested. Also to see the wild and gorgeous country he so deeply loved.

From Grand Canyon we went to Tuba City and Cameron, and talked with the Indian agents who had mailed out many bulletins in regard to Everett, with the hope of finding him . . . Then to Kayenta to talk with Mr. & Mrs. John Wetherill, who had conferred with him about travelling over the Karparowitz Plateau.

Somewhere in Arizona we had our first experience with a corduroy road, and we bounced and bounced right off into a field! We made an attempt to go to Rainbow Bridge, but got stalled for hours in a dry river-bed. We did not understand the necessary tire-deflation etc, and had no implements to dig ourselves out of the sand but our enamel saucers, a blanket and stray boards. Finally we got turned about and we backtracked, with no more ambition for Rainbow Bridge. I held on to the seat in fear at one point, as we climbed a high bare rock, and could hardly descry the road that we should follow as we descended by a sort of log stairway. We had to return by the same route; but, strange to say, it did not seem as frightening.

One day three drunken Indians careening along side on horseback, and asked us for whiskey . . . Another day/time we stalled on a road and found we were out of gas. We had to borrow of a bus driver who finally came our way. The reader will comment that we were very inexperienced travellers to go across Arizona, but our little Ford always carried us safely through.

June 25 We made a mistake in our road, so inquired of an Indian who was buying a sheep. He wore an American suit, but with many strands of beads around his neck, and a red headband. He spoke excellent English, so we invited him into our little one-seater. He was Edmund Nequativa, a Hopi ethnologist at the University at Flagstaff. We had a long talk about his education as a Christian in the government school in Phoenix. His father then concluded that a good Indian has the same high qualities as a good Christian, so why strive to make an Indian into a Christian, with much talk about hell?

Mr Nequativa was making an extensive study of the root words of various tribes of Indians, this collection of words being termed *Kerusian*. He said he would try to get information from the Navajos who had talked with Everett at Escalante Rim. One theory was that they might have arranged to row him across the Colorado River.

June 26 We had a pleasant visit at the Lowrey's place at Lee's Ferry. (They had been the first ones to write that our letters to Everett had been uncalled for early in the year.) On this June date, a robbery was reported and a wounded man had to be transported 150 miles to a hospital. Another man, barefooted and starving, was found in Kaibab Forest.

From the bridge, we thrilled at the deep gorge of the Colorado. We thought we recognized the very view Everett painted, and which we called "On and On and On" as printed on a folder with his "Wilderness Song."

In Kaibab Forest I loved the walk we took, threading our way between the trunks of the tall yellow pines, some only two feet apart. Their shadows stretched across the road. There were pinyons and junipers and elderberries too.

At 11 A.M. we crossed the line into Utah, hearing the sweet notes of a meadowlark. Tall lombardies and cottonwoods, and yellow flowers brightened the landscape.

In Zion Park, Mr. Mahan told us where to find Mr. Donal Jolly, the Chief Ranger, who had taken Everett to a hospital when he had a terrible case of poison ivy. His children had taken care of Everett's dog Curly, and there was a picture of him and his good adopted friends on the mantel. All the family were pleased to see the folio of watercolors we had carried with us.

We travelled along to see the wonders of Zion, and thanked the Mormons for giving them such meaningful names in their early time of refuge—The Gothic Arch, the Three Patriarchs, Sun Mountain, Virgin River, the Great White Throne, Angels' Rest, Shinwava Shrine, the Mount of Mystery, where we watched the last sunset glow.

We saw many sheltered spots where Everett probably slept, and the impressive Amphitheatre of great rocks with a drapery of green foliage and a natural pulpit in a pool of water. We felt sure that Everett had declaimed some well-loved lines to the surrounding vermilion cliffs.

We slept under the maples, with quite a wind blowing, but I wept a good share of the night. I felt so poignantly this haunting beauty that Everett loved, and the keen poison oak suffering that he had endured in this canyon. (In Indiana he had been through a similar case, but he was in a bed at home.) After climbing to see "Weeping Rock," I wrote a few lines—"I lay my grief before you," feeling that I need not weep again.

Down by the river in the morning, I made a colored pencil sketch of Lady Mountain and the slender aspens.

Back to Mt. Carmel, we turned toward Bryce Canyon, 64 miles distant. We ate lunch under cottonwoods, and saw silver poplars and locusts and dusty pines. At Ruby's Inn we interviewed Mr & Mrs Syrett, and Hal Rumel, who had attended Otis Art School and knew Everett.

Before sunset we visited Everett's friends the Copes—family of the Chief Ranger. The thirteen-year son Grant, named for the Mormon leader, rode around with us as guide, to show the famous pinnacles in their best light—the Arch, Temple, Organ, Queen Victoria, Queen's Palace, Dumb-bells, Art Gallery, the Pope etc. He also pointed to Navajo Mountain, which meant so much to Everett for its Indian mysteries . . . Grant had picnic supper with us, and explained why he did not desire to be Chief Ranger. He had won all his high school expenses by his high scholarship in the eighth grade . . . We had a cold night among the pines and Douglas firs.

June 28 We drove eastward to Tropic, where George Shakespeare, of famous forbears, shook hands feelingly with us over his rail fence. He wished he could go searching for Everett, as he had talked much with him. It was in this town that Everett took a boy with him to see the picture "Death Takes a Holiday." He had written home of liking the music very much. On one of his camp evenings, many boys gathered round to hear him singing with some Navajo Indians, after their supper of mutton and coffee. They had crossed the Colorado in order to buy some supplies.

We drove steeply to Escalante Rim, 9200 ft. elevation, and through some beautiful aspen glades that Everett often mentioned in letters. We met Mr Kester and Mr Griffin, sheepherders who knew Everett. We lunched under a fir of dense shade, and saw shrubs with pink blossoms. I held an aspen twig all the way as we drove to the little mountain town of Escalante.

Mr H. J. Allen, who had corresponded with us, met us in the street and invited us to his home for overnight. Chester Lay called, one of the searchers, and we went to see Mr & Mrs Harvey Bailey who had a new daughter. These men spoke of the large piece of Indian pottery which had been found in Davis canyon.

It was young Irene Allen who wrote, after seeing Everett's book in 1940, that she immediately read it twice over, with "swirlings of emotion." She wrote a school story about him, after asking us particulars about his childhood.

Next morning Mr Allen took us as far as his car could travel toward 66 Mile Mountain, so that we realized how difficult was Everett's burro-riding toward Davis Canyon, southeast. We wished that we had wings to fly.

At 4.30 P.M. we bade the Allens a grateful Good bye, and hurried to meet our dinner appointment at Panguitch with the 15 Civic clubs of southern Utah. They had financed one of the searching parties, and would continue their interest. Ida Chidester of the Deseret News interviewed me. Also Mr Ray Carr.

July 1 On our homeward way now we stopped at Bryce again. Grant Cope and I had an early morning horseback ride down the very steep path to the base of the canyon. My horse Bud seemed loath to go, but Grant coaxed him along. Grant pointed out the foxtail pines, picturesque and new to me. We saw primroses, flax and asters. Scenery from a horse's back is doubly interesting, while lights and shadows and colors change with every few steps. How grateful that I could ride!

That afternoon late we reached Cedar Brakes, 9900 ft. elevation, with a regular gale blowing, and patches of snow here and there. The aftershine of the sunset was like a streak of lightning along the edge of the lower clouds, with golden st[r]eaks above. We counted ridge after ridge of distant mountains, with red cliffs just below us. We built a fire in the cookstove of this tourist cabin of logs, and cooked rice and lentils. We were glad to have a snug evening to read and write and ponder our strange adventurings.

Back in Nevada we made a detour to see Lost City, partly reconstructed from an old Zuni village. We looked down into the Kiva, and climbed down a ladder into another room with a fire pit and roof-hole. We saw the Museum, where a Zuni Indian was mending old pieces of pottery.

[End]

Epilogue
by W. L. Rusho

Afterword
by Gary James Bergera

Epilogue
"Everett Ruess and His Footprints"
by W. L. Rusho

Everett Ruess once wrote, "When I go, I leave no trace," and told a librarian friend in 1934, "I don't think you will ever see me again, for I intend to disappear." As far back as 1932, he had written, "And when the time comes to die, I'll find the wildest, loneliest, most desolate spot there is." In the depression era of the 1930s, and within the lower forty-eight states, he could not have found a more lonely spot than the Escalante Canyon–Kaiparowits Plateau region of southern Utah—now the Grand Staircase–Escalante National Monument and the Glen Canyon National Recreation Area.

Everett Ruess did indeed disappear, almost as if he had vanished from the earth, during the cold months of 1934–35. Since that long-ago winter, journalists, historians, poets, students, and people young and old have pondered the possible fate of the young artist. Today, almost seventy years since, we are no closer to a definitive answer than were the searchers of the 1930s, but we can at least trace both the territory in question and the theories examined.

Everett's world of the early 1930s, not large in a global sense, was confined to his

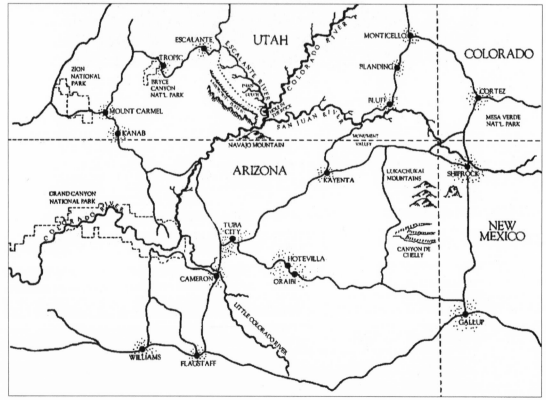

Everet Ruess Country

home state of California, to Arizona, and to the Four Corners region. Except for north-ern California, we would classify it all today as but a small portion of the American Southwest. Yet in a personal sense Everett's country is in fact immense, ranging from rugged alpine peaks to twisting desert canyons, from bubbling mountain streams to gleaming orange-red sandstone cliffs, including thousands of places to become lost or simply to disappear. As a young artist, Everett was attracted to known sites of color and dramatic topography, generally lands now set apart as national parks, monuments, or as tribal parks, and he visited several of them from 1930 to 1934. His final expedi-tion in November 1934 probed into southern Utah's Escalante River canyons, a com-plex arid region of vertical cliffs, plunging canyons, soaring mesas, slickrock, and sandy desert. Although undesignated as a protected area of the national park system until 1975, when the Glen Canyon National Recreation Area was established, the Escalante Canyon region possessed the colorful and dramatic visual elements Everett sought intensely as he entered his third decade of life.

During the 1930s, a person such as Everett Ruess could travel alone, even through national parks, rarely meeting other visitors. Particularly was this true in the lonely canyons of the Escalante River, where Everett apparently spent the last days of his life. On 11 November 1934, the young artist packed his few belongings into the packs of his two burros, waved good-bye to a few newly made friends in the town of Escalante, Utah, and headed southward into some of the most isolated and rugged lands in the nation. A week later he chanced upon two sheepherders, Clayton Porter and Addlin Lay, at their sheep camp near the head of Soda Gulch, an Escalante River tributary. Spending two nights at the camp, Everett told the men of his plan to paint and make sketches at Hole-in-the-Rock, overlooking Glen Canyon. Hole-in-the-Rock was the name given to that dramatically steep declivity down which Mormon pioneers on their way to settle in southeastern Utah drove eighty-three wagons toward a crossing of the Colorado River in January 1880.

After Everett left the sheepherders, and in the months and years that followed, sev-eral men and women in various locations reported either talking to someone who resembled Everett Ruess or discovering the supposed remains of his camp gear. But no one was ever able to verify seeing him alive. It was as if he had melded into the rust-red slickrock itself.

Everett had often written that he was heading into the wilderness and that he would not be sending letters home for two or three weeks. When he left Escalante, he wrote that he might be out of touch for as long as two months, and that he was headed toward Lee's Ferry, Arizona.

Stella and Christopher Ruess, in Los Angeles, when mailing letters to their son Everett, addressed them to the nearest post office to Lee's Ferry, which was Marble Canyon, Arizona. In February 1935, when the postmaster at Marble Canyon returned Everett's uncalled-for mail, Stella and Christopher were instantly alarmed, and they initiated a flurry of letters to Four Corners postmasters, sheriffs, federal officials, and Indian traders who might have knowledge of their son. The *Los Angeles Evening Herald* carried the story of Everett's disappearance on 14 February.

Postmaster Mildred Allen at Escalante, who had met Everett during his brief stay in town, turned over the letter she received to her husband, H. Jennings Allen, a

Garfield County commissioner, who alerted the community and organized a search party. On 1 March, searchers on horseback began combing through successive canyon tributaries to the Escalante River, but found nothing in Willow or Soda Gulches. Then on their descent down the single and steep slickrock trail into Davis Gulch, they spotted Everett's two burros grazing peacefully, kept in the canyon by a brush fence. In a nearby sheltered alcove, they discovered footprints, empty condensed-milk cans, candy wrappers, and marks left by a bedroll. Yet nowhere could the men find any of Everett's personal belongings—bedroll, cook kit, food, paintings, paint kit, journal, and money—all missing! How, without the aid of his burros, could Everett have carried it all out? On the fence hung a halter and a rope.

Did a searcher who found the burros and the halter, advance of the others, also find some or all of Everett's gear and simply appropriate it for his own use? As implausible as this seems, one of the searchers, Gail Bailey, in an August 1997 interview with moviemaker Diane Orr, reportedly admitted to taking Everett's belongings as well as the burros. If this is indeed true, it lends more weight to the probability that Everett died—either accidentally or by murder—on the Escalante side of the Colorado River.

An important point is that the 1935 searchers from Escalante confined most of their efforts to a *horseback* search; never is there an indication that they walked, climbed, or crawled up the many extremely deep and narrow side canyons inaccessible to a horse.

As the search party members continued down Davis Gulch, they examined alcoves containing small Anasazi ruins or petroglyphs. After climbing to a high small ruin in a shallow cave, the men stopped suddenly in surprise. There on the base of the doorway were carved the words NEMO 1934. Nearby were four Anasazi pottery jugs lined up on a flat rock. In another deep alcove containing numerous pictographs, these same words were found again, written in charcoal: NEMO 1934. Was this Everett's enigmatic signature?

Allen wrote to Stella and Christopher news of the discovery of the burros and asked if the NEMO inscriptions could somehow be associated with Everett. Their telegraph reply read:

> Everett read in desert Greek poem Odyssey, translated by Lawrence of Arabian desert. Here Odysseus, Greek word for nobody, "Nemo" being Latin for nobody. Odysseus trapped by man-eating giant in cave, saves life by trick of calling himself Nemo. Everett dislikes writing own name in public places. Mrs. Christopher G. Ruess

Later Christopher Ruess remembered that Everett had read and re-read Jules Verne's *Twenty Thousand Leagues Under the Sea*, in which Captain Nemo, like Everett, was depicted as trying to escape from civilization. This suggestion raised the possibility that Everett had disappeared intentionally.

Although he had earlier played around with a new name for himself, by 1934 he was back to using his given name. Of course, he had "escaped" from his winter sojourn in San Francisco, vowing never to return to a large city, but none of his later letters indicated any desire to break away from his past or to assume a new identity. His letters seemed cheerful and fully expectant that he would reach Lee's Ferry, where he would write again within a few weeks. Yet he had viewed this land from the slopes of Navajo Mountain, across the river. He had also looked down on it from the cliff tops of Bryce Canyon. Therefore, he must have realized that when he left the town of Escalante he was heading into a region of knife-cut, tortuous, convoluted, twisting, red-rock canyons, where finding a route to Lee's Ferry would be difficult. That he fully intended to return, however, and had made inquiries about possible routes is evident in his last letter to his parents:

> *I am going south towards the river now, through some rather wild country. I am not sure yet whether I will go across Smoky mountain to Lee's Ferry and south, or whether I will try to cross the river above the San Juan. The water is very low this year. I might even come back through Boulder.*

Ken Sleight, environmental activist, dude ranch owner, and former river runner, reported that during the 1960s he had seen a painted NEMO beside an Anasazi ruin in Grand Gulch, a southward flowing tributary of the San Juan River about forty miles east of Davis Gulch. Sleight said that above the NEMO was an abstract painting on the rock. Years later, when Sleight again visited the inscription, he found that it had been obliterated, either by someone trying to erase "graffiti" or by the natural erosion of weather. Since the only other NEMO inscriptions were in Davis Gulch, Sleight theorized that Everett learned of the many ruins in Grand Gulch from archaeologists he had worked with in Arizona, that he made his way to Grand Gulch in late 1934, only to perish somewhere on his return to Davis Gulch. "Perhaps he drowned while trying to swim the Colorado River," Sleight conjectured.

Since learning that Everett, after a dreadful backpacking experience in 1930, never again went backpacking overnight away from his pack animals, apparently never even carried a backpack or knapsack, and that he had a debilitating anemia (discussed in further detail later), Sleight has since revised his conjecture to conclude that Ruess probably never left the area near Davis Gulch.

Randolph "Pat" Jenks, who, as a young man had befriended Everett in 1931, believes that Everett did indeed journey southward, across the Colorado River, but that he was probably killed by hostile Paiute Indians who then lived near Navajo Mountain. Jenks said that when he (Jenks) was on a hiking trip to Rainbow Bridge in the 1930s, his Navajo guide became alarmed when he spotted some distant Paiutes. "Hurry!" the Navajo shouted to Jenks. "If they catch us, they kill us! They kill all strangers!"

Implicit in all the correspondence between Allen and the Ruesses was the supposition that Everett may simply have fallen from a high precipice and, that in the complex and jagged topography, no one had yet found the body. Anyone acquainted with the character of the country would suggest falling as a possible solution. Everett himself had written, "Hundreds of times I have trusted my life to crumbling sandstone and nearly vertical angles in the search for water or cliff dwellings," and "Yesterday I did some miraculous climbing on a nearly vertical cliff, and escaped unscathed. . . . One way and another, I have been flirting pretty heavily with Death, the old clown." Since the 1935 search party never investigated the very narrow upper side canyons, this suggestion holds considerable merit.

In spite of the strong possibility of falling, the fact remains that for sixty years hikers and photographers have looked into every twist of the Escalante's canyons, but no body was ever found. Of course, a flash flood could have destroyed all evidence.

Another theory states that Everett may have accidentally witnessed an act of small-scale cattle rustling, which was known to have occurred in the Escalante Canyon area. Perhaps he witnessed a rustler kill a cow, then brand the cow's calf—or simply trail a cow and calf out of the Escalante River area. If a nervous, possibly paranoid, rustler saw Everett at the time, he may have killed Ruess to silence a potential witness. At least one known cattle thief was reported to have said he shot young Ruess, with details on how he and two others disposed of the body in the Colorado River. But this man, found in a state of apparent senility in 1983 (a senility later denied by the man's son), said he knew nothing of Everett's disappearance.

Well-known outdoor writer David Roberts interviewed several older citizens of the town of Escalante, Utah—people who had either met Everett in 1934 or knew of local cattle rustling episodes during the early 1930s. In a feature article entitled "What Happened to Everett Ruess?" in *National Geographic Adventure* (Spring 1999), Roberts appeared convinced that Everett probably met his fate at the hands of rustlers. To follow up a report that rustlers crossed the Colorado River at a place called Jackass Bench (about 1.5 miles north of Hole-in-the-Rock), Roberts, on a hot July day in 1998, hiked along the canyon rim until he found the old cairn-marked trail down the sandstone slickrock to Lake Powell. Then backtracking to the top of the trail, he discovered three strange saw-cut logs, some tin milk cans, and, most importantly, a strange mound of sand and rock that Roberts thought could be Everett's grave—or a hiding place for Everett's journal and other belongings. Roberts said he started to dig into the mound, then turned away, because, he said, "I realized that it wasn't really the pile of rocks that I most wanted to leave undisturbed—it was the mystery of Everett Ruess."

In May 1999, with my wife, Carole, my grandson, Nathan Wallace, and friend, Don Cecala, I investigated the mysterious Jackass Bench Trail, found the three logs, a milk can, and the mound. Convinced that the mound could not be a grave, we tentatively began discarding rocks and loose sand. But within twenty minutes of digging to a depth of about eighteen inches, we found only sandstone bedrock! Apparently the mound had been formed by a natural disintegration of a small sandstone hoodoo, leaving sand covered by broken slabs of rock. It was not a grave; neither was it a repository for Everett's journal and camp gear.

Back in 1935, Jennings Allen conjectured that perhaps Everett had taken his belongings to the top of Kaiparowits Plateau, but a lengthy search of that long lofty mesa to the west produced nothing.

If Everett left intentionally and did somehow carry his belongings out of Davis Gulch (and if he did not head for Grand Gulch), he could have possibly joined Navajo traders who had crossed the Colorado River to trade in Escalante and were on their return south. In Everett's 11 November letter, he mentions having met Navajos near the town of Escalante and that he "stayed up most of the night, talking, eating roast mutton with black coffee and singing songs." In this scenario, he could have been deceived into leaving voluntarily only to be murdered by an Indian somewhere south of Davis Gulch. Since he did not take his burros, however, he would have to have been invited by the Navajos, with the assurance that they would bring him back later—a rather improbable scenario.

In the summer of 1957, however, three archaeologists working on the Glen Canyon Archaeological Survey prior to the filling of Lake Powell were examining Cottonwood Canyon when they came across the remains of camping equipment. Among the items found were a rusty cup, spoon, fork, kettles, pans, and a large canteen. Most interesting was a box of razor blades labeled Owl Drug Store, Los Angeles. Cottonwood Gulch (now named Reflection Canyon on Lake Powell maps) lies only about eight to ten miles southeast of Davis Gulch and would have been along the path toward a crossing of the Colorado River. The camp equipment was sent to Stella Ruess, but Stella said she doubted that it belonged to Everett. Nevertheless, one wonders why generally indispensable camp equipment would be abandoned eighty miles from the nearest town, unless, of course, someone was trying to hide evidence. Perhaps Stella merely wanted to believe that the gear was not Everett's.

On 13 March 1953, the *Salt Lake Tribune* reported the discovery, by ranchers, of two small shacks, food, and camping equipment about forty miles south of Tropic, Utah. Because several of the food cans were rusted through, it was estimated that the camp had been abandoned about twenty years earlier, or about the time Everett had visited Davis Gulch. The *Tribune* article conjectured that this might have been the last camp of young Ruess, yet three facts go against that theory: (1) Clothing found in the shacks was for a small man, only about 5 feet tall, while Everett was 5 feet 10 inches tall. (2) The camp site was on the west side of the tall and rugged Kaiparowits Plateau, while Davis Gulch is on the east side, a separation of at least fifty air miles.

A logical route between the two places would have taken Everett through the town of Escalante, where he surely would have been recognized. (3) Everett's burros were found in Davis Gulch, so they could not have been used to transport camp gear over or around the lofty plateau. This theory is hardly tenable.

Stella and Christopher Ruess did everything they could to locate their missing son, but all their attempts failed. Through their efforts and those of Jennings Allen of Escalante, a second search was made of the Escalante Canyon area, but it turned up only the second NEMO inscription and a few footprints, nothing more.

The Ruesses were victimized by a cruel, scheming con man and outlaw named Neal Johnson, who called himself "Captain Johnson." (Johnson said he had been commissioned a captain in the Mexican Army.) Johnson took money from Christopher and Stella on the pretext that he would hire three Navajo Indians to scour the Indian country south of the Colorado River. Although Johnson sent letters and telegrams back to the Ruesses indicating that he was hot on Everett's trail, he in fact found nothing—if he really conducted any search whatsoever. Yet upon Johnson's insistence that Everett might be in the Navajo country, the Salt Lake Tribune sent one of their star reporters, John Upton Terrell, with Johnson on a tour through the Navajo Reservation to talk with Indians and white traders. For eleven days their progress—or lack of it—was reported by Terrell in the *Tribune*, but no trace of Everett was ever found.

In June 1935, Stella and Christopher toured southern Utah and northern Arizona, stopping to talk with anyone who had met Everett, or who had known of his passing, including national park superintendents and rangers, businessmen, postmasters, and county officials. In the town of Escalante, they met Jennings Allen and talked with most of the members of the search party as well as young people who had befriended Everett during his short visit.

In 1976 a nearly complete skeleton was discovered in a boat in a garage on the south rim of Grand Canyon. The garage and boat had belonged to the late and well-known photographer-explorer named Emery Kolb, who had probably discovered the bones somewhere along the Colorado River, brought them home, but apparently never told anyone about his find. After Kolb died, the bones were found and turned over to the Coconino County sheriff, who, in turn, sent them to the Human Identification Laboratory at Arizona University in Tucson. Dr. Walter Birkby, now retired, made several attempts to identify the skeleton, but without success. A search through the Kolb photographs now archived at Northern Arizona University disclosed no photo of the skeleton in situ, and no reference to where the bones had been found. Adding to the mystery was the fact that the skull had a bullet hole in the right temple and the bullet itself was lodged in congealed tissue. Analysis showed that the bits of clothing with the skeleton could have dated from the 1920s or 1930s. Could the bones be those of Everett Ruess? Probably not, since Dr. Birkby said that the individual would have been at least 6 feet tall, while Everett, as stated earlier, was only 5 feet 10 inches. Furthermore, the skeleton was of a man who had been heavy boned and quite muscular, possibly employed as a miner. Everett, on the other hand, shunned hard work like the plague.

Mark Taylor, author of *Sandstone Sunsets: In Search of Everett Ruess* (Salt Lake City: Gibbs Smith, Publisher, 1997), a book that deals tangentially with Everett's disappearance, makes the conjecture—based, as the author states, on "unsubstantiated evidence"—that Emery Kolb may have been gay or at least bisexual. On the same type of evidence, Taylor further suggests that while on a photographic trip to southern Utah, Kolb killed Everett for rejecting his advances. Furthermore, he believes the skeleton in Kolb's boat was only 5 feet 7 inches tall and could indeed have been Everett. When contacted about this theory, Dr. Birkby had only one word: "Hogwash!"

In a 1991 monograph, The *Kolb Brothers of Grand Canyon*, published by the Grand Canyon Natural History Association, author William C. Suran states:

> *The truth about the skeleton comes to light in Emery's diaries and letters. Emery had found the bones in a prospector's pit many years earlier, while exploring the gorge between Bright Angel Trail and Grandeur Point.*

What is not generally known is that Everett suffered, at least at times, from a debilitating disease. On 21 July 1932, he wrote in his journal,

> *Physically I feel weak. I would not be surprised to hear that pernicious anemia had hit again. A slight bruise has taken three weeks to heal. My injured toe will pain me for weeks to come. Diet more trouble.*

This brief note would help explain why Everett was often lethargic, why he avoided hard work and tired so easily. It would also explain his frequent bouts of depression

Everett, taking a moment to relax.

and thoughts of death. Pernicious anemia, essentially a deficiency of hemoglobin in red blood cells, was long a mysterious malady with no apparent cause. Hence, it was termed "pernicious" and was, over several years, almost always terminal. In the late 1940s, pernicious anemia was found to be caused by a lack of vitamin B-12, or cobalamin. Vitamin B-12, found only in meat, cannot be utilized by people lacking glycoprotein in the stomach, which was probably Everett's condition. Today the problem can be cured by regular injections of B-12. Gary James Bergera, in his afterword, suggests that Everett may have suffered from a malady similar to B-12 deficiency, perhaps folic acid deficiency. Yet whatever the cause, the symptoms were essentially the same.

To attempt psychological speculation of unproven validity, an examination of his existing journals and letters might indicate that Everett had a bi-polar disorder, perhaps a manic-depressive condition causing mood swings alternating between deep depression and ecstatic, joyful happiness. A series of Everett's melancholy jottings, as Bergera has assembled, might even suggest suicide, but it tends to neglect the happier episodes that Everett also describes.

Theories arise and are discarded when they don't fit existing facts. The truth is that we simply don't know, and will probably never know, the fate of young Ruess. We have some of his 1934 letters, but they read more like crafted essays than chatty letters. What were his intentions? And where is his 1934 journal? Everett had once written that the "lone trail is the best for me" and "In the meanwhile, my burro and I, and my little dog, if I can find one, are going on and on, until, sooner or later, we reach the end of the horizon."

The goals and the dreams of Everett Ruess, as well as his solitary sojourns into mountain or red-rock wilderness, are perhaps better appreciated today than they were when he disappeared. Rarely in the literature of the canyon country does one encounter the sensitive, thoughtful, sincere, and emotional imagery found in Everett's letters. We have come to realize that the lands of the canyon country are finite and fragile, and that Everett's ability to articulate his artistic vision can even today help us to understand our own feelings and experiences as we follow his footsteps through the almost ineffable color and grandeur of Nature's pageant.

Afterword

"'The Murderous Pain of Living': Thoughts on the Death of Everett Ruess"

by Gary James Bergera

My name is nemo [no one]. My parents call me nemo, as do all my companions.
— Odysseus, *The Odyssey*

Almighty God! Enough! Enough!
— Captain Nemo's "Last Words,"
Twenty Thousand Leagues Under the Sea

I am exploring southward to the Colorado, where no one lives.
— Everett Ruess, [19–21?] November 1934

NEMO 1934.
— Everett Ruess's last words

For many readers of Everett Ruess's remarkable letters home, a terrible melancholy permeates almost every line. Born on 28 March 1914, the 5-foot 10-inch, 150-pound dreamer was just four months shy of his twenty-first birthday when he disappeared, virtually without a trace, southeast of Escalante, Utah, in November 1934. He had spent the better part of the previous four years tramping, starry-eyed and often alone, through the mountains and deserts of the American Southwest, hoping to satisfy a hungry aestheticism. During the weeks and months away from his Los Angeles home, he chronicled his worship of nature in more than a hundred letters to his parents, Christopher and Stella, his older brother, Waldo, and a handful of friends. Some were no more than pencil scratches on a postcard; others filled pages. Most were evocative, heartfelt celebrations of a life lived on its own harrowing terms. Published in part in 1939 and 1940 and more fully in 1983, the letters have moved hundreds of thousands of readers with their haunting meditations on the universal quest for solitude, freedom, and understanding. Because of them we easily forgive Everett's "callow romantic[ism],"[114] and remember him not as hopelessly incompetent or self-indulgent, but as the embodiment of our own youthful idealism.[115]

From Everett's revealing correspondence, it is tempting to speculate that the young poet knew even before he first left home as a precocious sixteen-year-old bound for intense adventure that he would one day succumb to what he called "the murderous pain of living."[116] To date, the three most likely explanations for Everett's disappear-

106

ance are (1) he died falling from a cliff, drowning in a river, or becoming lost in a canyon maze; (2) he was murdered by white cattle rustlers or local renegade Native Americans; or (3) he trekked south into Arizona or Mexico and lived beyond 1934.[117] In what follows I would like to explore another possibility and suggest that Everett, depressed, battling health problems, and perhaps wrestling with his own sexuality, may have committed suicide. I realize that such psychologically oriented discussions are difficult enough for the living, let alone the dead, and that even at their most cautious they are highly speculative. I am also aware of the danger that, because such analyses tend to focus on dysfunction, they may achieve little more than reduce their subjects to one-dimensional caricatures. This is certainly not my intention. While I focus on particular aspects of Everett's character at the exclusion of others, I personally find him a charming, albeit troubled young writer of considerable promise whose death is a tragedy we will never fully explain. Finally, I appreciate that such studies may actually reveal as much—if not more—about their writers, or the times during which they write, as about their subjects. With these important caveats firmly in mind, I believe that what emerges from a careful review of Everett's writings is a portrait of a gifted yet depressive young artist whose tortured engagement with life both powered his creative expression and propelled him toward his own self-destruction.[118]

I

I went to the woods . . . because I wished to live deliberately, to front only the essential facts of life, and see if I could not learn what it had to teach, and not, when I came to die, discover that I had not lived.
—Henry David Thoreau

Beauty's nothing / but the beginning of Terror we're still just able to bear, / and why we adore it so is because it serenely / disdains to destroy us.
—Rainer Maria Rilke

Everett Ruess is most accessible to us today through his letters, journals, poems, essays, and stories—some 175,000 words—as well as his blockprints and watercolors. His letters, articulate and insightful, became his "principal vehicle of expression" during his wilderness wanderings. While the letters "offered an assured, sympathetic audience," they also gave voice to his overwhelming feelings of awe and allowed him to create a persona that better reflected the image he had—or wanted to have—of himself. Finally, their careful "drafting and polishing"[119] suggest that Everett may have sanctioned a more probing analysis of their possible meaning.

Even before his first extended solo foray into the California mountains,[120] Everett was drawn to the romance of the "deserted field." This is especially apparent in his early adolescent poems "The Relic," "Two Arrowheads," "The Indian Council Cave," and "Pledge to the Wind." In 1930, at age sixteen and with his parents' blessing,[121] he headed alone up the California coast to Carmel and Big Sur, then on to Yosemite and the Sierra Nevada. His chatty letters home only hint at the "blue moods" his later writings would disclose.[122] "[T]here is no thrill from riding," Everett wrote after this first trip, "that can compare to the delight of swinging sturdily along a winding forest trail. Whenever I consider trails[,] a strange, deep longing fills me to be rambling on a curving pathway."[123] He also composed four new poems at this time: "Colors I've Failed to Catch," "Life Is a Song," "My Life Shall Be a Little Curling Wave," and "My Soul Set Free." (The latter two contain the earliest known allusions to his own death.)

Upon graduating from high school in January 1931, Everett, increasingly convinced he could find true happiness only in the wilderness, left for Monument Valley on the Utah-Arizona border. In view of his age and inexperience, this act appears "genuinely foolhardy,"[124] yet it is also in keeping with his reckless approach to danger. Off and on for the next three and a half years, Everett, blissfully oblivious to his own shortcomings, traveled the deserts, canyons, and mountains of northern Arizona, southwestern Colorado, eastern California, northwestern New Mexico, and southern Utah virtually penniless and alone except for a pack burro or two and a stray dog he adopted.

After Monument Valley, Everett trudged southeast to Canyon de Chelly and the San Francisco Peaks in Arizona, then northwest to the Grand Canyon. After a brief excursion to Zion National Park, he returned to the Grand Canyon, then on to the Salt River Valley and Superior, Arizona, before returning home to Los Angeles that December. The next year, 1932, he was back in Arizona, where he visited the Salt River Valley again, Roosevelt, Ganado, and Canyon de Chelly before heading northeast to Mesa Verde, Colorado, then southwest back to the Grand Canyon. That September he enrolled in the University of California at Los Angeles but dropped out early in 1933. From June to October he hiked the Sierra Nevada, camping in Sequoia and Yosemite National Parks. In October he relocated to San Francisco, which he hoped would be more conducive to his creative temperament. By the next March, however, he had decided to return to the desert. From Monument Valley, he ventured west to Navajo Mountain and Rainbow Bridge, then southeast to Gallup, New Mexico, continuing west to the Grand Canyon, Flagstaff, Oak Creek Canyon, and the Grand Canyon again. In October he moved north into Utah, where he visited Bryce Canyon National Park, then passed east to the villages of Tropic and finally Escalante.

Everett's passion for nature and blossoming skill as a writer are perhaps most evident in a letter he wrote in May 1934, six months before his disappearance. "[T]he other night at twilight, unwilling to drown my consciousness in slumber, and dissatisfied with life, I packed and saddled my burros, and left my camp by a rushing stream at the edge of the desert," he began.

> *The half moon had an orange glow as I rode on the trail up the mountains. Behind us, thunder boomed on the open desert, and black clouds spread. Moaning winds swept down the canyon, bending the tops of the tall pines and firs, and clouds hid the moon. Silently old Cockleburrs, my saddle burro, carried me upward through the night, and Leopard followed noiselessly with the pack. Grotesque shapes of trees reared themselves against the darkening sky, and disappeared into the blackness as the trail turned.*
>
> *For a while the northerly sky was clear, and stars shone brilliantly through the pine boughs. Then darkness closed upon us, only to be rent by livid flashes of lightning, and thunder that seemed to shake the earth. The wind blew no*

longer and we traveled in an ominous, murky calm, occasionally slashed with lightning. Finally the clouds broke, and rain spattered down as I put on my slicker. We halted under a tall pine, and my sombrero sheltered the glow of a cigarette. The burros stood motionless with heads down and water dripping off their ears.

In half an hour the rain was over and the skies cleared. By moonlight we climbed to the rim of the mountain and looked over vast silent stretches of desert. Miles away was the dim hulk of Shiprock—a ghostly galleon in a sea of sand . . . Oh but the desert is glorious now with marching clouds in the blue sky, and cool winds blowing. The smell of the sage is sweet in my nostrils, and the luring trail leads onward.[125]

After leaving Escalante on Sunday, 11 November 1934, Everett followed the old Hole-in-the-Rock trail southeast toward the Colorado River and Davis Gulch, site of his last-known camp. On the nineteenth, he chanced upon two sheepherders and spent the next two nights with them. As they were heading back to town on the twenty-first, Everett handed them a letter to his brother, Waldo, and asked if they would mail it. "I think there is much in everyone's life that no one else can ever understand or appreciate, without living through the same experiences, and most could not do that," he confided in what would be the last letter he ever wrote. That is why "I've become a little too different from most of the rest of the world. . . . I have not tired of the wilderness," he continued; "rather I enjoy its beauty and the vagrant life I lead, more keenly all the time. . . . Do you blame me then for staying here, where I feel that I belong and am one with the world around me?" Despite attempts at friendship and a "civilized" life, Everett had come to realize he could never "settle down. I have known too much of the deeps of life already, and I would prefer anything to an anticlimax." He admitted, "Often as I wander, there are dreamlike days times[126] when life seems impossibly strange and unreal." It had been "a full, rich year," he reminisced, adding that he had "left no strange or delightful thing undone that I wanted to do." From there, he vowed, he would continue south, "where no one lives."[127]

II

To die in the open, under the sky, far from the insolent interference of leech and priest, before this desert vastness opening like a window onto eternity—that surely [would be] an overwhelming stroke of rare good luck.
— Edward Abbey

I should like to disappear into the very depths of the wilderness and be alone. I should like to go where the silence is a profound noise and a human footprint is only the dust blowing in the wind behind me . . . I should like to look, perhaps to see something of eternity in the distance to the horizon . . .
— Michael Terry Hurst (1943–1979)
Epitaph 1968, Blanding City Cemetery, Utah

W. L. Rusho, Everett's editor and biographer, is a cautious interpreter.[128] He doubts that Everett simply walked away from his last camp, since he "remained too close to his parents and to his brother" to have severed "all communication—forever."[129] Nor does Rusho necessarily favor death by accident or murder.[130] As he knows, the two most compelling pieces of evidence against the latter are the presence in Davis Gulch of Everett's two burros and the absence of his personal possessions. Everett's burros were found in a natural corral, healthy and reasonably well-fed. But almost all of his personal belongings were missing—the exceptions being a bridle, halter, and rope. If Everett had been murdered, why did the killer(s) leave his riding outfit and pack animals? If he had died in an accident, what happened to his blankets, clothes, money, camera, painting supplies, pictures, food, diary, etc.? If he had died somehow and someone later come across his belongings and taken them, why didn't they take his burros and riding gear, as well?[131] If Everett wanted to cross the Colorado, some ten miles away, and continue south, how did he plan to transport his provisions?

When searchers entered Davis Gulch in early March 1935, all they found besides Everett's burros and riding gear was the word "NEMO"—Latin for "no one"—scratched onto an Indian ruin and on a rock wall.[132] At first, Everett's parents wondered if NEMO referred to Odysseus, since they knew Everett had read T. E. Lawrence's 1932 prose translation of Homer's epic adventure, *The Odyssey*.[133] Trapped in a cyclops's cave, Odysseus refuses to reveal his true name to the one-eyed monster, thereby saving his own life and those of most of his crew when the cyclops, now blind, can only say that "no one"—"No-man," according to Lawrence—had attacked him. Thus, his parents guessed, Everett may have come to see himself as a romantic adventurer escaping the barbarians of modern civilization, or simply as a "no one" to everyone he had once loved.

Another possibility is that Everett was alluding to Captain Nemo, commander of the submarine *Nautilus* in French writer Jules Verne's fantastic romance *Twenty Thousand Leagues Under the Sea*.[134] According to his parents, Everett had read the book several times, and his own copy was "well worn." Nemo explains early in the novel, "I'm not what you would call a civilized man!" and "I've broken with all of society for reasons which I alone can appreciate. I therefore don't obey its rules . . ." A little later: "[O]ne must live—live within the ocean! Only there can one be independent! Only there do I have no master! There I am free!"[135] In the sequel, *The Mysterious Island*, which Everett had read in late 1928,[136] Nemo, "that great misanthropist," was filled by the "whole civilized world . . . with such disgust and horror" that "he wanted to leave it forever."[137]

Such statements would have resonated with Everett, and Rusho wonders if he, "like Nemo, felt that he had suffered too many defeats. He could have felt depressed and withdrawn, notwithstanding cheerful posturing in his letters."[138] "Whatever the cause," Rusho continues, Everett's "withdrawal from organized society, his disdain for worldly pleasures, and his signatures as NEMO in Davis Gulch, all strongly suggest that he closely identified with the Jules Verne character."[139] Everett was, Rusho concludes, "still impressionable, still able to project himself into idealistic, if unrealistic, roles. Could Everett have consciously determined that he would disappear, that he would 'break every tie upon earth,' so as to turn into Nemo himself?"[140]

"Everett's letters occasionally foreshadow his death or disappearance," Rusho admits, "almost as if he were making plans for one, or perhaps both, of these eventualities."[141] He reports that when Everett left California for the last time for Arizona in 1934, he bade "goodbye to [Alec W.] Anderson [a retired librarian from Covina, California], then added, as an afterthought, 'And I don't think you will ever see me again, for I intend to disappear.'"[142] But Rusho never pursues the possibility that Everett killed himself.[143] True, he wonders if Everett "may have believed that he was failing, as an artist, to live up to his parents', and his own, expectations."[144] But for Rusho this probably meant that he had been "harboring, perhaps for years, a growing determination to strike out on his own, by cutting all ties to his parents," not that he was suicidal.[145]

Others have not been so reticent. Ironically, in his introduction to Rusho's biography, novelist John Nichols writes: "I picture [Everett] simply expiring on the edge of a sandstone cliff, in the shadow of some high circling buzzard, convinced that he could never again return to civilization."[146] There "this tormented and eloquent pilgrim was engulfed and erased by the territory whose mysteries had absolutely conquered his entire being."[147] Fourteen years later journalist Alex Shoumatoff ventured: "A final possibility is that Ruess climbed way up some cliff, settled into an alcove or down on some ledge out of sight from below, and, having no further interest in living, simply checked out, and his remains haven't been found yet."[148]

III

Please don't be distressed because I'm the way I am. Just be grateful that I'm so much happier than most people and trying to go on an up-climbing curve, rather than marking time with those who have come from the regulation mold.
—Richard Halliburton

If you want to get more out of life . . . you must lose your inclination for monotonous security and adopt a helter-skelter style of life that will at first appear to you to be crazy. But once you become accustomed to such a life you will see its full meaning and its incredible beauty.
—Christopher McCandless

Within the last twenty years, science has finally begun to outline the broad contours of the complex interplay between creativity and mental dysfunction.[149] "The fiery aspects of thought and feeling that initially compel the artistic voyage," writes Kay Redfield Jamison, "commonly carry with them the capacity for vastly darker moods, grimmer energies, and, occasionally, bouts of madness.'"[150] In fact, adds Arnold M. Ludwig, "members of the artistic professions or creative arts as a whole . . . suffer from more types of mental difficulties and do so over longer periods of their lives than members of the other professions."[151] For Everett Ruess, such distress may have manifested itself as alternating episodes of depression and hypomania (a mild form of mania) separated by periods of considerable normalcy—symptoms that today might indicate cyclothymia, often a precursor to manic depression.[152] These and other mood disorders afflict as many as 15 million Americans annually, less than a third of whom are diagnosed as such. Tragically, their suicide rate is thirty-five times that of Americans generally.[153]

In his writings Everett revealed an expansive euphoria that could last days, weeks, and sometimes longer, as well as other symptoms of hypomania, such as irritability, grandiosity, sleeplessness, talkativeness, and racing thoughts.[154] "Alone on the open desert," he wrote in 1931, "I have made up songs of wild, poignant rejoicing and transcendent melancholy. The world has seemed more beautiful to me than ever before."[155] "I myself feel much freer and happier here than I did in the city," he added the next day, "but that is due not only to a change in environment, but to a change in my mental attitude."[156] "Once more I am in the desert that I know and love," he recorded the next year,[157] reporting that "[t]he beauty of the wet desert was overpowering."[158] Three weeks later he had "[shaken] off my melancholy, gathered flowers under the red cliffs and chanted poetry in the hogan." He "wanted to write," his thoughts raced, but he admitted that "the words would not come."[159]

Alone, he could be at his most delirious: "Then up the starlit road between the pillared redwoods," he enthused in 1933. "I munched chocolate and sang at the top of my voice . . . some Dvorak melodies. The forest boomed with my rollicking song. Then the transmuted melodies of Beethoven, Brahms, and the Bolero . . . [I] swung exultantly down the white pathway to adventure."[160] "[E]very once in a while I feel quite ecstatic," he told his family the next week. Unfortunately, "I slip out of such moods quite easily."[161] Such confessions alarmed his parents. "No, I am in no danger of a nervous breakdown at present," he quipped the year before his death. "How about you?"[162] By the end of that summer he was "so happy and filled to overflowing with the beauty of life, that I felt I must [tell you. . . . It is all] a golden dream, with mysterious, high, rushing winds leaning down to caress me, and warm and perfect colors flowing before my eyes. . . . A gentle, dreamy haze fills my soul, the rustling of the aspens lolls my senses and the surpassing beauty and perfection of everything fills me with quiet joy and a deep pervading love for my world."[163]

The next year, again in the open desert, he found himself "[o]nce more . . . roaring drunk with the lust of life and adventure and unbearable beauty." "I've been so happy," he gushed, "that I can't think of containing myself." "To live is to be happy," he exulted, "to be carefree, to be overwhelmed by the glory of it all. Not to be happy is a living death."[164] "Even when to my senses the world is not incredibly beautiful or fantastic," he stated, "I am overwhelmed by the appalling strangeness and intricacy of the curiously tangled knot of life, and at the way that knot unwinds, making everything clear and inevitable, however unfortunate or wonderful."[165] The beauty of this country is becoming a part of me," he confessed in late June 1934, adding that he felt "detatched [sic] from life and somehow gentler."[166]

Everett's writings also contain expressions of extreme physical activity, poor judgment, and exaggerated self-confidence, additional features of hypomania.[167] "I like adventure and enjoy taking chances when skill and fortitude play a part," he once bragged. "Many times in the search for water holes and cliff dwellings, I trusted my life to crumbling sandstone and angles little short of the perpendicular, startling myself when I came out whole and on top."[168] Such recklessness was not without its repercussions, and Everett suffered a number of problems, including following false leads or getting lost,[169] chasing runaway burros (sometimes at night),[170] almost being gored by wild bulls,[171] enduring debilitating bouts of poison ivy,[172] eating poisoned food,[173] and getting stung by bees.[174] Everett also intensely disliked sleep, which he called "temporary death," and sometimes went seventy hours without sleeping.[175]

At the same time, Everett manifested the unmistakable signs of depression, including a loss of pleasure and energy, difficulty sleeping, fatigue, lethargic or agitated speech, problems with diet, difficulty concentrating, and repeated thoughts of death and suicide.[176] "Somehow I don't feel like writing now, or even talking," he confided in 1931, knowing that he sounded "incoherent and inconsistent," that "thoughts are jangling within me."[177] At the onset of an extended trip through Arizona the next year, he worried that the adventure "was foredoomed to failure, that I'd be overcome with melancholy if I visited the places I've seen before . . . I've drifted too far away from other people. I want to be different anyhow; I can't help being different, but I get no joy from it, and all common joys are forbidden me."[178] Life on the road "has much more uncertainty than it would have at home," he confessed. "The low spots are fearfully low, but I have learned that they do not last, and a few glorious moments make me forget them completely."[179] "I felt futile . . .," he confided two weeks later. "I am losing contact with life."[180] Such "long thoughts" prevailed over the next several days. "I think I have seen too much and known too much," he told himself, "so much that it has put me in a dream from which I cannot waken and be like other people." He thought of a poem by Robinson Jeffers—"Who goes too far to find his grave, / Mostly alone he goes."[181]

"I am only too readily led into a melancholy mood," he acknowledged the next year.[182] A week later he recorded thinking that "the value of life is not much. At any given moment, you are only going thru the motions, not living. Working blindly at routine, holding pointless conversations, and the like are not living, yet it is such things that make up our existence."[183] By the end of that summer he had come to "despise confirmed dudes, tenderfeet, mollycoddles, and sloppy campers. There are no words for my feeling. . . . Even if I cannot paint," he told himself, "at least I have the sense of beauty, which these and [other] campers lack completely."[184] Three months later his mood turned even darker: "Often I am tortured to think that what I so deeply feel must always remain, for the most, unshared, uncommunicated. Yet, at least I have felt, have heard and seen and known, beauty that is inconceivable, that no words and no creative medium are able to convey. Knowing that the cards are stacked, and realized achievements are mere shadows of the dream, I still try to give some faint but tangible suggestion of what has burned without destroying me." He wrote stoically, "When events are over, it is often easier to trace the inevitability of their course. Have you not found it so? It is a genius, however, who can find in the past what will serve to plot the future. Most of us must wait until things have happened to see why they happened, and even then, we often do not see."[185]

"I have been in a very restive, unstable mood, and did not feel like writing," he told his brother in late 1933. "I have been discovering new moods, new lows, new and disturbing variations in myself and my feelings for individuals, and people as a whole.

. . . [F]or the most part there has been an undercurrent of resentment or unrest . . . I have not been able to loosen up for some while." He lamented not finding "any proper outlet for my feelings. Perhaps there is none and perhaps it is necessary for my feelings to die of weariness and refusal." "I don't expect you to understand them [my emotions] any more than anyone else," he despaired, "nor would it matter much if you did, because it seems to be up to me." He knew his "straying from normalcy" was disturbing but hoped it was simply "part of a somewhat symmetrical scheme which I seem to see dimly."[186] Six months later his outlook had not improved: "I fear, or rather, the rest of the world should fear, that I am becoming quite antisocial. I have no desire to bend my efforts toward entertaining the bored and blase world. . . . I hope this gets you down," he complained, "for I feel like puncturing the stupid satisfaction and silly aspirations of the world this morning. . . . Beauty has always been my god," he railed; "it has meant more than people to me. And how my god, or goddess, is flouted in this country, which to me is the most beautiful I've known in all my wanderings! . . . Living in the midst of such utter and overpowering beauty as nearly kills a sensitive person by its piercing glory, they are deaf, dumb, and blind to it all."[187]

Like these admissions of depression, explicit references to his own death also began emerging by 1931. "[B]efore physical deterioration obtrudes," he told his brother that year, "I shall go on some last wilderness trip, to a place I have known and loved. I shall not return."[188] "[W]hen the time comes to die," he repeated in 1932, "I'll find the wildest, loneliest, most desolate spot there is."[189] "I set less and less value on human life, as I learn more about it," he confessed the next year. "Life does not grip me very powerfully in the present . . . I don't like to take a negative attitude, but it seems thrust upon me." "My interest in life is waning," he wrote the next week.

"What's the use?" he lamented by the end of the month. "All perishes—why struggle?"[190] In fact, Everett soon began to think of death as the artist's true destiny: "[H]e who has looked long on naked beauty may never return to the world. . . . Alone and lost, he must die on the altar of beauty." "[S]ometimes, if his will is powerful, [the "highly sensitive person"] can pretend to himself that he does not know what he knows," Everett wrote just six months before his death, "and can act a part as one of the rest. But the pretense cannot endure, and unless he can find another as highly strung as himself with whom to share the murderous pain of living, he will surely go insane."[191] "Mine seems a task essentially futile," he admitted. "Try as I may, I have never yet, that I know of, succeeded in conveying more than a glimpse of my visions . . . I am torn by the knowledge that what I have felt cannot be given to another. I cannot bear to contain these rending flames," he moaned, "and I am helpless to let them out. So I wonder how I can go on living and being casual as one must."[192]

Contributing to such anguish was Everett's inability to form lasting friendships. Again in 1931, a year out of high school, he complained of not having "a loyal friend to share my delights and miseries."[193] He called himself "freakish" because he could not find "people who cared about the things I've cared for."[194] "I can't find my ideal anywhere," he lamented the next year. "So I am rather afraid of myself."[195] Yet he could be uncompromising of what few acquaintances he did have: "They have been wallowing in the shallows of life this past year," he complained in early 1934, "not growing or having new and enlarging experiences; driven partly or wholly by circumstances into lives that they themselves consider ignoble, stale, and depressing."[196] He concluded that true friendship was impossible. "I do not greatly mind endings, for my life is made up of them," he wrote four months later, "but sometimes they come too soon or too late, and sometimes they leave a feeling of regret as of an old mistake or an indirect futility. . . . [F]or the deepest understanding," he thought, "one must seek those with whom one can be most truly one's self." Yet for Everett, this meant not human intimacy but experiencing "the nearly unbearable beauty of what I see."[197]

Compounding Everett's psychological battles were health problems. "Physically I feel weak," he wrote in 1932. "I would not be suprised to hear that pernicious anemia had hit again."[198] Prior to the 1940s, most cases of anemia (also called "tired blood"[199]) were usually grouped in one category. Today they are separated and classified according to the body's failure to absorb vitamin B-12 (pernicious anemia), iron, or folic acid. In each case, however, the symptoms are similar: weakness and fatigue, dizziness, and pale skin (including gums, eyes, and nailbeds), as well as, less often, palpitations, shortness of breath, red tongue, loss of appetite, abdominal problems, and depression.[200] Vitamin B-12 deficiency, usually unrelated to diet, is rare and affects people primarily over age fifty and of northern European or African descent.[201] More common among adolescents is folic acid deficiency anemia, usually the result of a diet lacking raw leafy vegetables. In fact, "anemia due to folic acid deficiency looks just like pernicious anemia . . . [and] careful diagnostic tests must be performed to distinguish between the two."[202] Iron deficiency anemia affects 10 to 30 percent of adults in the United States and may be more common among young men than previously believed.[203] Still, it is important to remember that "most fatigue is not related to tired blood; most anemia comes on without any noticeable symptoms at all . . ."[204] A more common ailment of adolescents is infectious mononucleosis, whose symptoms, like anemia, include weakness and fatigue.[205]

Of Everett's sexual orientation, writer Mark A. Taylor was the first to wonder if his traveling alone was an attempt "to understand his own sexuality."[206] As Everett's readers know, this complex question is difficult to answer. On the one hand, he was clearly interested in a woman from San Francisco with whom he "was intimate" and shared "some moments of beauty." He also referred in his letters to "a very interesting Polish girl,"[207] another woman who was "quite attractive to me,"[208] a third "who was very interesting to me,"[209] a "Mormon girl" he would have "fallen in love with" had he stayed in town "any longer,"[210] and captioned a photograph of a Navajo woman, baby, and himself, "My Navajo Wife."[211]

On the other hand, Everett once signed a letter to a friend, "Love and kisses, Desperately yours,"[212] and the following year described a young man who spoke with him as "six feet three, [and] rather handsome."[213] Another time a young man "wanted to sleep with me, outside." The next morning Everett wrote of having "had an ugly dream about him."[214] Everett's use of the word "ugly" may have a sexual connotation. In a third instance, Everett recorded liking a young man who had "delicate, handsome features." Together, they and another friend "came to a spring in some buckeyes, filled pails, and climbed back . . . It was a glorious experience for me," he reported.[215]

Everett told his brother that in Hollywood he had known "several people with fine orthophonic victrolas and whole cabinets full of symphonies, but all these people were

115

either offensively[216] queer[217] or impossible in some other way, so I did not hear their music."[218] Yet eight months later, writing from Hollywood, Everett confided to a friend: "I have several friends with fine victrolas and recorded music, and I have some myself and can borrow more."[219] In another letter he hinted at "strange comradeships and intimacies,"[220] and seemed to allude to a sexual encounter when he wrote in mid-1934: "True, I have had many experiences with people, and some very close ones, but there was too much that could not be spoken. I had a strange experience with a young fellow at an outpost, a boy I'd known before. It seems that only in moments of desperation is the soul most truly revealed. Perhaps that's why I am so often so unrestrained, for always I sense the brink of things."[221] Everett doubted he would ever find "a great and soul-filling love," which "is such a rarity as to be almost negligible."[222] And when talking about his ideal companion, he did so without reference to gender: "I wish I had a companion, some one who was interested in me. I would like to be influenced, taken in hand by some one, but I don't think there is anyone in the world who knows enough to be able to advise me. I can't find my ideal anywhere. So I am rather afraid of myself."[223]

Taken together, these cycling bouts of depression and hypomania, exacerbated by possible health problems and questions about his sexuality, may have formed the "somewhat symmetrical scheme" which Everett in late 1933 "seem[ed] to see dimly."[224] That he sensed the problems he faced and their likely resolution is suggested in an eerily prophetic short story he completed two years before his death. [225] As it opens, an artist is "sprawled on the stinging hot sand beneath a twisted Joshua tree in the desert." He had come there to "die—or to recover his lost ambitions." Despite the beauty around him, his "soul was dead." With the approach of dawn, "he threw himself down in a little gulch beneath an overhanging ledge." "I'm a fool," he said, "but after all, what is the use of anything?" Soon, however, his physical discomfort became "greater than his spiritual misery,"[226] and the "desire to live was suddenly reawakened." He turned and began to run back, but "each step became a hammer blow at his heart." With his "last ebbing strength," he crawled "atop a lonely butte." Rain burst from the sky, and "[t]he dull misery that had been the artist's was washed away like the sand that poured down from the rocks, leaving them clean, and bare to the open sky." As his strength "waned, somehow, his happiness grew greater. He knew he could not get back, but he was content."[227] Vultures began circling, and "[a]ll that was left of his anguish now passed, and a light shone in his eyes, as he saw the dying sun flood the waste lands with splendor." The last thing he saw was the "burnished bronze of the vulture's wings, glinting in the sunlight, as it snatched his eyes out. He did not feel the pain. A moment later, the bloodhued sunset passed swiftly to night."[228]

". . . we learned of the many cliff dwellings [Everett] had seen, and of his precarious climbs to some high isolated ones."

V

Being alone had made me realize that man is pretty insignificant in the universe, like a speck of dust.

—Robin Lee Graham

We live unsettled lives / And stay in a place / Only long enough to find / We don't belong.

—Mark Strand

When "the murderous pain of living" finally became too much, and the end arrived, perhaps it happened this way: Everett led his two burros to the campsite in Davis Gulch. From there he explored nearby side canyons, cliffs, and buttes, until he found a wild, lonely spot that reminded him of a place he had been before. Returning to Davis Gulch, he loaded his outfit onto one of the burros and led him back to this spot. After unloading his pack, Everett walked the burro back to Davis Gulch. He removed the riding gear, left it nearby, made sure both animals were protected and had enough food for the winter, and hiked back to his last camp.

Two years earlier, in Canyon del Muerto, Everett had hidden an old saddle high "in a prehistoric corn bin beside a cliff-dweller's cradle . . . to be guarded by the spirits of the ancient dead." He wrote, "I don't think anyone will ever find the saddle. The rain washed away my tracks. The saddle is well cached. The ghosts of the cliff dwellers will guard it."[229] With this same thought in mind, Everett now gathered up his gear, all the beauty he had carried with him, and secured it in a recess he knew no one would ever find.[230] Slowly with the setting sun, the misery and anguish of the past four years began to wash away and Everett felt life loosen its grip. From this altar of beauty, he gazed one last time across the horizon. Content that he had kept his dream, Everett knew he was now going to make his destiny.

Whatever his fate, for Everett Ruess at the end there was only one word that he believed best summed up his brief life, one word that today tantalizes as it repels: nemo, no one. Like Odysseus, he found himself a prisoner in a foreign land facing a monster that threatened to devour him. Like Captain Nemo, he had fled the soul-deadening horrors of civilization only to discover that life held no choice but to become the thing he despised. Alone in his ravishing desert where "no one [*nemo*] lives," enveloped by transcendent beauty and the inescapable realization that he would never rise above the limits of his own flawed humanity, he believed he could do nothing else but become no one. For each new generation that confronts the same murderous pain of living, perhaps there is only one final word as well: Everett.

The older person does not realize the soul-flights of the adolescent. I think we all poorly understood Everett.

—Christopher Ruess

Endnotes

[1] These are "Letter from War God Spring" in *Desert Magazine* 2 (January 1939): 5; "I Have Stayed with the Navajo" in *Desert Magazine* 2 (February 1939): 15; "Southwest Wilderness Journeys" in *Desert Magazine* 2 (March 1939): 15–16; "170-Mile Walk on the Desert" in *Desert Magazine* 2 (April 1939): 25–26; "Vagabond of the Desert Wilderness" in *Desert Magazine* 2 (May 1939): 7; "With Archaeologists at Basketmaker Cave" in *Desert Magazine* 2 (June 1939): 9–10; "1127 A.D. in Arizona" in *Desert Magazine* 2 (July 1939): 29; "I Drove Away Countless Hordes of Evil Spirits" in *Desert Magazine* 2 (August 1939): 11; "Tragedy in the Canyon of Death" in *Desert Magazine* 2 (September 1939): 24, 30; five separate selections in an article entitled "I Have Really Lived" in *Desert Magazine* 2 (October 1939): 17; and "I Have Not Tired of the Wilderness" in *Desert Magazine* 2 (November 1939): 29.

[2] Originally published in *Desert Magazine* 1 (September 1938): 18.

[3] Originally published in *Desert Magazine* 1 (September 1938): 18–20.

[4] Actually, Everett's letter of 11 November 1934 to his parents was mailed from Escalante, Utah.

[5] "Youth Is for Adventure" dates this to 1928; see also a letter from Stella Ruess to Everett, 12 March 1928, in which she compliments his new poem, "The Relic." Photocopies of previously unpublished Ruess materials are in the possession of Gibbs Smith, Publisher, in Layton, Utah.

[6] Also printed in *L.A. Daily News*, 10 May 1935; in A Vagabond for Beauty, 26.

[7] The *L.A. Daily News* and *A Vagabond for Beauty* render this "Or chanting solemn prayers, in gay attire."

[8] The *L.A. Daily News* and *A Vagabond for Beauty* render this "And here the silent centuries invade."

[9] In *A Vagabond for Beauty*, 10–11.

[10] "Youth Is for Adventure" dates this to 1929.

[11] Originally published as the first of five selections in an article entitled "I Have Really Lived" in *Desert Magazine* 2 (Oct. 1939): 17; in *A Vagabond for Beauty*, 39–40.

[12] Everett used both "Lan" and "Lan Rameau" during this period as occasional pen names. "Lan" referred to the French *l'âne*, for ass, donkey, burro; hence, "Lan Rameau," Rameau the ass. "As to the burro," he wrote to his family, "I call him Everett, to remind me of the kind of person I used to be" (*A Vagabond for Beauty*, 37; see also 219n4, 25, 29, and 30). "Rameau" probably came from *Le Neveu de Rameau (Rameau's Nephew)*, a satire of eighteenth-century French manners by Enlightenment *philosophe* Denis Diderot, which Everett may have read in high school French classes. In this short, perplexing work, published after Diderot's death, Rameau's nephew, also called Rameau, is described as: "He shakes things up, he creates a stir; he makes people approve or disapprove; he brings out the truth; he makes you see who the decent people are; he unmasks the rogues. It is at such times that the man of good sense keeps his ears open and makes a note of who is who." Later, however, he is called "a loafer, a glutton, a coward, and rotten through and through." See *Diderot's Selected Writings*, ed. Lester G. Crocker, trans. Derek Coltman (New York: The Macmillan Co., 1966), 113–46.

[13] In *A Vagabond for Beauty*, 40–41.

[14] Only the second paragraph and poem are in *A Vagabond for Beauty*, 44–45.

[15] Chinle, Arizona.

[16] Everett's burro.

[17] Originally published as "170-Mile Walk on the Desert" in *Desert Magazine* 2 (April 1939): 25–26; in *A Vagabond for Beauty*, 48–49.

[18] The other young man was Tad Nichols.

[19] In the original, as well as in *A Vagabond for Beauty*, this sentence reads, "He enjoyed the puppy biscuits greatly."

[20] *A Vagabond for Beauty* renders this "The next two days."

[21] In *A Vagabond for Beauty*, 56–58.

[22] *A Vagabond for Beauty* dates this 27–28 August.

[23] *A Vagabond for Beauty* renders this paragraph differently.

[24] In A *Vagabond for Beauty*, 58–59.

[25] *A Vagabond for Beauty* says 30 September.

[26] Titled "A Rainbow Glowed for a Moment . . ." in the 1950 second edition; in *A Vagabond for Beauty*, 60–63. According to the original, this is one letter written at two different times on the 9th.

[27] Pericles, one of Everett's burros; the other was Pegasus.

[28] The second clause of this sentence is not in the original.

[29] In *A Vagabond for Beauty*, 63–64.

[30] "Youth Is for Adventure" and *A Vagabond for Beauty* both say 23 October.

[31] Everett eventually chose the names Cynthia and Percival. See the next letter.

[32] Originally published as the second of five selections in an article entitled "I Have Really Lived" in *Desert Magazine* 2 (October 1939): 17; titled "Idyllic Days in the Aspens . . ." in the 1950 second edition; not in *A Vagabond for Beauty*.

[33] This would have been in early August 1931; see *A Vagabond for Beauty*, 54.

[34] See the woodcut in *A Vagabond for Beauty*, 68.

[35] "Youth Is for Adventure" renders this last line as "Best wishes for a blithesome Noel."

[36] In *A Vagabond for Beauty*, 67–68.

[37] Only the first paragraph is in *A Vagabond for Beauty*, 70.

[38] Originally published as the third of five selections in an article entitled "I Have Really Lived" in *Desert Magazine* 2 (October 1939): 17; in *A Vagabond for Beauty*, 143, though not treated there as a letter.

[39] "Youth Is for Adventure" capitalizes Wild.

[40] Originally published as "Tragedy in the Canyon of Death" in *Desert Magazine* 2 (September 1939): 24, 30; last six-and-a-half paragraphs in *A Vagabond for Beauty*, 83.

[41] This episode is found in Everett's diary, 21–22 July 1932, and in *Wilderness Journals*, 70–73.

[42] The original reads "baby board."

[43] The original reads "I don't think I'll buy another horse . . ."

[44] The original reads "I don't think anyone will find the saddle."

[45] In his diary Everett rendered this name "Evert Rulan." "Rulan" is probably a play on "Ruess," mispronounced "Roo-ass" (instead of Roo-ess), perhaps as an echo of adolescent teasing, and then Frenchified to "Ru-lan," *l'âne* again meaning ass or burro. Everett's father did not care for his son's various *noms de plume*, and was glad when Everett eventually abandoned them. See his letter to Everett, 30 July 1930.

[46] The original reads "I don't think I'll return for it tho."

[47] In *A Vagabond for Beauty*, 87–89.

[48] Only the last three sentences of the second to last paragraph appear in *A Vagabond for Beauty*, 70.

[49] Probably the fall, when he enrolled at UCLA. After one semester, he did not return.

[50] Originally published as "Southwest Wilderness Journeys" in *Desert Magazine* 2 (March 1939): 15–16; not in *A Vagabond for Beauty*. Several of the following paragraphs appeared earlier in an essay, dated 30 September 1932, that Everett wrote for his freshman English class at UCLA.

[51] Arizona.

[52] In *A Vagabond for Beauty*, 93–96.

[53] *A Vagabond for Beauty* says 23 March 1933.

[54] Not in *A Vagabond for Beauty* as such.

[55] See "Tragedy in the Canyon of Death": "An Indian was whistling a herd of sheep."

[56] See "Wilderness Journeys of 1932": "After months in the desert and months in the city, I long for the sea caves, the breakers crashing in the tunnels, the still tropicolored lagoons, the jagged cliffs and ancient warrior cypresses."

[57] See "I Am Going to Shoulder My Pack": "I rode a black horse on the cool velvet beach at the edge of the surf, splashing through the salt water at times, and galloping beside the waves."

[58] In *A Vagabond for Beauty*, 97–98.

[59] Everett mentions his encounters with members of the Civilian Conservation Corps in his diary for this period.

[60] In *A Vagabond for Beauty*, 104–5.

[61] Titled "Canyon Trails by Moonlight . . ." in the 1950 second edition; in *A Vagabond for Beauty*, 98–99.

[62] Everett records in his diary on 2 July 1933 receiving a letter from Lawrence Janssens, so a date of July 1933 for this reply may be more accurate. The 1950 second edition renders Janssens's given name as "Laurence."

[63] Not in the 1950 second edition. According to his diary, Everett had met Ned Frisius and Charley Hixson, two vacationing Hollywood High School students, on 14 July 1933. He left them one week later on 21 July.

[64] In *A Vagabond for Beauty*, 102–3.

[65] *A Vagabond for Beauty* says the recipient is Doris Myers, the date 30 August, and the location Castle Crags. In his diary for 30 August 1933, Everett mentions writing letters but does not identify Myers as one of his addressees.

[66] *A Vagabond for Beauty* renders this concluding paragraph differently.

[67] Not in the 1950 second edition. The date is 4 December 1933, according to *A Vagabond for Beauty*, 119.

[68] For his father's response, dated 10 December 1933, see *A Vagabond for Beauty*, 120–23.

[69] In *A Vagabond for Beauty*, 180–81. According to "Youth Is for Adventure," Everett spent two years working on this poem, finishing it in 1933.

[70] The *L.A. Daily News* version reads: "In cool sweet-grasses I have lain alone, . . ."

[71] Paragraph originally published in "Everett's Home" in both the first and second editions of *On Desert Trails with Everett Ruess*; title and reference added here; full letter in *A Vagabond for Beauty*, 129–32.

[72] Paragraph originally published in "Everett's Home" in both the first and second editions of *On Desert Trails with Everett Ruess;* title and reference added; full letter in *A Vagabond for Beauty*, 133–34.

[73] Originally published as "Vagabond of the Desert Wilderness" in *Desert Magazine* 2 (May 1939): 7. Not in *A Vagabond for Beauty* as such, yet compare his letter to Frances, 149–51.

[74] First paragraph originally published as the fourth of five selections in an article entitled "I Have Really Lived" in *Desert Magazine* 2 (October 1939): 17; in *A Vagabond for Beauty*, 140–42.

[75] In *A Vagabond for Beauty*, 145–46.

[76] In *A Vagabond for Beauty*, 146–48.

[77] Originally published as "I Have Stayed with the Navajo" in *Desert Magazine* 2 (February 1939): 15, minus paragraphs 1, 2, 10, 11, 12, 13, 18, and 19; in *A Vagabond for Beauty*, 152–55.

[78] *Desert Magazine*, as well as "Youth Is for Adventure," identified the recipient as Bill Jacobs.

[79] Originally published as "Letter from War God Spring" in *Desert Magazine* 2 (January 1939): 5, minus paragraphs 6, 9, 10, 13, 15, and 16. Earlier publication in "Here's History of Strange Disappearance at Outpost" in the *Salt Lake Tribune,* Sunday, 25 August 1935, 10, 12. In *A Vagabond for Beauty*, 158–61.

[80] *Desert Magazine*, as well as "Youth Is for Adventure," date this letter 12 June; *Salt Lake Tribune* and *A Vagabond for Beauty* both say 29 June.

[81] This paragraph and the preceding one appeared first in the *Salt Lake Tribune* and then in *A Vagabond for Beauty* but not in either edition of *On Desert Trails*.

[82] In *A Vagabond for Beauty*, except the last paragraph, 161–64; *Vagabond* prints this letter as two separate letters, the first to his parents, the second (the second and third to last paragraphs) to "Addressee unknown."

[83] In *A Vagabond for Beauty*, 156–58. The recipient is Carl Skinner.

[84] Originally published as "With Archaeologists at Basketmaker Cave" in *Desert Magazine* 2 (June 1939): 9–10; in *A Vagabond for Beauty*, 165–66.

[85] *A Vagabond for Beauty* renders this concluding paragraph differently.

[86] Originally published as "1127 A.D. in Arizona" in *Desert Magazine* 2 (July 1939): 29.

[87] Compare *A Vagabond for Beauty*, 163.

[88] Treated as one postcard in the 1950 second edition; in *A Vagabond for Beauty*, 169 (first postcard), 169–70 (second postcard).

[89] In *A Vagabond for Beauty*, 170, and dated 10 September.

[90] Originally published as "I Drove Away Countless Hordes of Evil Spirits" in *Desert Magazine* 2 (August 1939): 11; in *A Vagabond for Beauty*, 171.

[91] In *A Vagabond for Beauty*, 175–76, and dated 4 November.

[92] In *A Vagabond for Beauty*, 176–77.

[93] Actually, this was probably the second to last letter Everett wrote. See the next letter.

[94] According to his mother, Everett sent home a total of twenty pictures.

[95] *Desert Light* appears as the frontispiece in the 1940 and 1950 editions of *On Desert Trails*.

[96] Originally published as "I Have Not Tired of the Wilderness" in Desert Magazine 2 (November 1939): 29, and dated "a few days before he departed on his final journey." In *A Vagabond for Beauty*, 178–80, and dated 11 November. The original carries only the month, with a question mark for the day, suggesting that Everett did not know what day it was. The first paragraph, and a second that was reprinted in *Vagabond* but not in *On Desert Trails*, appeared earlier in "Here's History of Strange Disappearance at Outpost" in the *Salt Lake Tribune*, Sunday, 25 August 1935, 10. Rusho correctly believes this was the last letter Everett wrote. His parents believed it was the next to last.

[97] The second paragraph, which appeared in the *Salt Lake Tribune* and later in *A Vagabond for Beauty* but not in *On Desert Trails*, reads: "I know that I could not bear the routine and humdrum of the life you are forced to lead (in the city). I know I could never settle down. I have known too much of the deeps of life already, and I would prefer anything to an anticlimax." *Vagabond*, as well as the original manuscript, render the second sentence "I don't think I could ever settle down."

[98] Originally published as "What Became of Everett Ruess?" in *Desert Magazine* 2 (December 1939): 9–11, 37.

[99] Rusho disputes this; see *A Vagabond for Beauty*, 186.

[100] Originally published as "Is Everett Ruess in Mexico?" in *Desert Magazine* 2 (December 1939): 10; not in the 1950 second edition.

[101] Hugh Lacy, "Say That I Kept My Dream . . . ," *Desert Magazine* 1 (September 1938): 18–20.

[102] Originally published as "Letter from Tad Nichols" in *Desert Magazine* 2 (June 1939): 10.

121

[103] "170-Mile Walk on the Desert," *Desert Magazine* 2 (April 1939): 25-26; in *A Vagabond for Beauty*, 48–49.

[104] Hugh Lacy, "What Became of Everett Ruess?" *Desert Magazine* 2 (December 1939): 9–11, 37.

[105] A third literary connection to Nemo is in Charles Dickens's 1852–53 novel, *Bleak House*. Chapters 10 and 11 recount the story of Nemo (which the text explains is Latin for "no one"), a scrivener, or copyist, employed by the legal profession. Nemo may not have been his real name, but "it's the name he goes by." He is described as "black-humoured and gloomy," has no friends, and "keeps himself very close." He is discovered dead in his small apartment, the victim of an opium overdose. It is unclear if his death was intentional or accidental.

[106] Not in the 1950 second edition.

[107] Stella Knight Ruess died in 1964.

[108] Christopher Ruess died in 1954.

[109] This was not updated in the 1950 second edition. These awards are no longer offered.

[110] The first paragraph of this letter is in *A Vagabond for Beauty*, 151, the second is not. In addition, the version in *Vagabond* has two different concluding paragraphs. Finally, *Vagabond* says this letter is addressed to "[Addressee unknown"] and is dated May 1934.

[111] Again, Rusho disagrees; see *A Vagabond for Beauty*, 186.

[112] This may overstate both Everett's possessions and their value.

[113] This second installment explains that Everett rode one burro and used the second as a pack animal.

[114] In *Mormon Country*, 321.

[115] In *Glen Canyon and the San Juan County*, western historian Gary Topping prefaces his own recent treatment of Everett with the following comment: "So much paper and ink have been expended on Ruess, especially on speculations regarding his mysterious disappearance from an Escalante side canyon in 1934, that it almost seems an environmental crime to add to the expenditure" (317). See bibliography on page 128 for an overview of material written about Everett Ruess; some of these sources are cited in abbreviated form in this afterword.

[116] Portion of an untitled essay, quoted in a letter to Edward Gardner, May 1934; see *A Vagabond for Beauty*, 148.

[117] His father, Christopher (*A Vagabond for Beauty*, 206), and journalist John Terrell (see the *Salt Lake Tribune's* reports, referenced on pages 74–93) believed that Everett had been murdered. In 1952, however, his parents reportedly said they thought he died while trying to cross the Colorado River (see Leap, "Utah Canyons Veil Fate of L.A. Poet," 2).

[118] This approach differs from that which sees Everett as having "cleansed himself of society's expectations and, in a way, transformed himself into a deeper, more complete, and more fulfilled person" (Taylor, *Sandstone Sunsets*, 37, 55). Furthermore, it should be clear to readers of his epilogue that W. L. Rusho questions the main argument of the following discussion. While I share Rusho's concerns and agree that we will never know what happened to Everett, I believe that the written record Everett left behind deserves our serious consideration and that psychology offers an approach that should not be ignored.

[119] *A Vagabond for Beauty*, 9.

[120] Everett had visited the Sierra Nevadas and Yosemite several times before the summer of 1930.

[121] "The thing for you to do," his father had counseled several years earlier, "is to stick to your hobbies, whether art, or naturalist's interest, or chemistry, and so know just what you are going to college for. . . . If you find yourself now you have a head start on all who wait till they are grown up to begin to start to prepare. Think this over" (Christopher to Everett, 26 October 1927, previously unpublished).

[122] See letter to Father, Mother, and Waldo, 22 August 1930; also in *A Vagabond for Beauty*, 23. Everett's salesman father had hoped that the experience away from home, which he thought was "fully equal to any course at High School," would help Everett learn how to "meet people and *desire to please*

them, which is the act of personal charm. If you don't learn instinctively to *desire to please* you will not develop charm. After all, charm and personality and most of these fine things are just forms of unselfishness, thoughtfulness for others" (Christopher to Everett, 30 July 1930, emphasis in original, previously unpublished).

123 "Trails," Hollywood High School theme, 1930, in "Youth Is for Adventure."

124 *A Vagabond for Beauty*, 26; see also Topping, *Glen Canyon*, 317–18.

125 Letter to Frances (surname unknown), May 1934, in *A Vagabond for Beauty*, 149–51.

126 This is mistranscribed as "tinges" in *A Vagabond for Beauty*, 180.

127 Letter to Waldo, "November the ? [19–21?] 1934 Escalante Rim, Utah"; see *A Vagabond for Beauty*, 178–80, 184.

128 See *A Vagabond for Beauty*, 182–213.

129 Ibid., 208.

130 See ibid., 190, 195–97. "It is just about as difficult to see how Everett Ruess could have been murdered," Wallace Stegner had opined forty years earlier, "as it is to see how he could have got out of the Escalante Desert" (*Mormon Country*, 329). As Rusho points out and dismisses in his epilogue, one of the most inventive explanations holds that Everett may have been killed by Emery Kolb, famous longtime guide to the Grand Canyon and environs. Periodically, other stories surface of eyewitness accounts of or confessions to Everett's murder (see, for example, David Roberts's recent "What Happened to Everett Ruess?" and compare Rusho's response in his epilogue). Such folklore, originating in and fueled by frontier braggadocio, is notoriously unreliable. Proof, such as remnants of Everett's personal belongings, would contribute significantly to verifying such reports. To date, however, none of Everett's possessions has ever turned up.

131 Mark Taylor reports that one of the members of the original Ruess search party, boasted of having proof that Everett's belongings had been found at the time. When Taylor pressed him, he agreed to show him what he had but never showed up for their meeting (*Sandstone Sunsets*, 17, 109; see also Roberts, "What Happened to Everett Ruess?").

132 According to Rusho (*A Vagabond for Beauty*, 188), members of the Ruess search party found the word NEMO inscribed twice, first on the wall of a cave and then a mile away on the doorstep of an ancient Indian stone house. He adds that one of the searchers told Everett's parents they also found the words "Nov 1934" carved in stone not far from the Indian house. More recently, Mark Taylor (*Sandstone Sunsets*, 10) has asserted, without documentation, that searchers found a longer message, "NEMO was here. Nov. 1934," carved in a "soft sandstone wall." Photographs of the two NEMO inscriptions show only the words "NEMO 1934" (*A Vagabond for Beauty*, 187, 189).

133 See *The Odyssey of Homer, Newly Translated into English Prose*, by T. E. Shaw [T. E. Lawrence] (New York: Oxford University Press, 1932). It is unclear how Everett could have known from *The Odyssey*, a Greek poem translated into English, that nemo is Latin for "no one." Perhaps he encountered the word in a high school Latin class or in reading different translations of *The Odyssey*. His father had written to him in 1932: "Read the Odyssey, as I am now, in one translation, whether you get it all or not, then if you like it, read it again in another translation, and maybe the third translation you read you may want to read footnotes. When I have read this edition by my old teacher, I will send it to you, . . . The Odyssey is extraordinarily simply, perfect, lovely, natural, in deed a work of art" (Christopher to Everett, 5 July 1932).

134 *A Vagabond for Beauty*, 210.

135 Jules Verne, *Twenty Thousand Leagues Under the Sea*, trans. Anthony Bonner (New York: Bantam Books, 1962), 69, 74.

136 Everett Ruess Diary, 11 November 1928.

137 Jules Verne, *The Mysterious Island*, trans. and abr. Lowell Bair (New York: Bantam Books, 1970), 198, 196.

138 *A Vagabond for Beauty*, 210. While Verne's Nemo was suicidal, he did not feel he had suffered

too many defeats; rather, he was overcome by the knowledge that he had embraced the violent evil he had vowed to combat.

[139] Ibid., 211.

[140] Ibid. As previously noted, a third literary connection to nemo may be found in Charles Dickens's 1852–53 novel, *Bleak House*.

[141] *A Vagabond for Beauty*, 211.

[142] Ibid.

[143] *A Vagabond for Beauty*, 208.

[144] Ibid., 210.

[145] Rusho has since raised the possibility of suicide, but is skeptical. See *Wilderness Journals*, 15.

[146] *A Vagabond for Beauty*, x.

[147] Ibid., xi.

[148] Shoumatoff, *Legends of the American Desert*, 16.

[149] "[T]here is strong scientific and biographical evidence linking manic-depressive illness and its related temperaments to artistic imagination and expression" (Kay Redfield Jamison, *Touched with Fire: Manic-Depressive Illness and the Artistic Temperament* [New York: The Free Press, 1993], 240). For a more clinical discussion of depression, see Frederick K. Goodwin and Kay Redfield Jamison, *Manic-Depressive Illness* (New York: Oxford University Press, 1990). See also Arnold M. Ludwig's comprehensive *The Price of Greatness: Resolving the Creativity and Madness Controversy* (New York: The Guilford Press, 1995). A good general treatment of mood disorders is Peter C. Whybrow, *A Mood Apart: The Thinker's Guide to Emotion and Its Disorders* (New York: Basic Books, 1997).

[150] Jamison, 2; see also 41, 47–48, 102.

[151] Ludwig, 4.

[152] See Jamison, 14.

[153] See Whybrow, 7, 18; see also 291.

[154] These symptoms are summarized from James Morrison, *DSM-IV Made Easy: The Clinician's Guide to Diagnosis* (New York: The Guilford Press, 1995), which in turn relies on *Diagnostic and Statistical Manual of Mental Disorders*, 4th ed. (Washington, D.C.: American Psychiatric Association, 1994).

[155] Letter to Bill Jacobs, 18 April 1931; see *A Vagabond for Beauty*, 39–40. Years earlier Everett's father had written: "You have a good mind. Now you need to observe *people* as you observe *things* and learn to make many *friends*. Try to please people. You are a little like your daddy, who gets so interested in ideas at times that he is absentminded about people. That is bad. Because people have feelings" (Christopher to Everett, 30 September 1926, emphasis in original, previously unpublished).

[156] Letter to Waldo Ruess, 19 April 1931; see *A Vagabond for Beauty*, 41.

[157] Letter to Bill Jacobs, 20 June 1932; see *A Vagabond for Beauty*, 72.

[158] Everett Ruess Diary, 1 July 1932, in *Wilderness Journals*, 54.

[159] Ibid., 21 July 1932, in *Wilderness Journals*, 71.

[160] Ibid., 11 June 1933, in *Wilderness Journals*, 109; compare *A Vagabond for Beauty*, 99.

[161] Letter to Family, 16 June 1933; see *A Vagabond for Beauty*, 101.

[162] Letter to Family, 5 July 1933; see *A Vagabond for Beauty*, 101.

[163] Letter to Doris Myers, 30 August 1933; see *A Vagabond for Beauty*, 102–3.

[164] Letter to Bill Jacobs, 5 May 1934; see *A Vagabond for Beauty*, 145–46.

[165] Letter to Edward Gardner, May 1934; see *A Vagabond for Beauty*, 147.

[166] Letter to Bill Jacobs, 29 June 1934; see *A Vagabond for Beauty*, 160–61.

[167] *A Vagabond for Beauty*, 26. See, for example, letter to Waldo, 9 October 1931, in ibid., 61; letter to Bill Jacobs, 13 November 1931, in ibid., 64; and letter to Waldo, 13 December 1931, in ibid., 66.

168 Letter to Emily Ormond, 2 May 1934; see *A Vagabond for Beauty*, 140, 142. "This time in my wanderings I have had more reckless self-confidence than ever before," he added the next month. "Hundreds of times I have trusted my life to crumbling sandstone and nearly vertical angles in the search for water or cliff dwellings." Letter to Carl Skinner, June 1934; see *A Vagabond for Beauty*, 157. See also letter to Ned Frisius, 27 September 1934; see *A Vagabond for Beauty*, 171. A young archaeologist whom Everett met in 1934 remembered that he "seemed careless about his own safety when climbing around cliffs" (*A Vagabond for Beauty*, 165. See also letter to Family, 25 Aug. 1932; see *A Vagabond for Beauty*, 87).

169 See letter to Waldo, 11 November 1934; see *A Vagabond for Beauty*, 179.

170 Letter to Father and Mother and Waldo, 18 August 1931; see *A Vagabond for Beauty*, 56; letter to Emily Ormond, 2 May 1934; see ibid., 141–42.

171 Letter to Edward Gardner, May 1934; see *A Vagabond for Beauty*, 146–47.

172 See letter to Bill Jacobs, 27–28 August 1931; see *A Vagabond for Beauty*, 56.

173 Letter to Bill Jacobs, 17 June 1934; see *A Vagabond for Beauty*, 153.

174 Letter to Waldo, November 1934; see *A Vagabond for Beauty*, 178.

175 Everett Ruess Diary, 28 August 1933, in *Wilderness Journals*, 171; see *A Vagabond for Beauty*, 102; see also letter to Frances (surname unknown), May 1934; see *A Vagabond for Beauty*, 149; for sleeplessness, see Everett Ruess Diary, 8 October 1933, in *Wilderness Journals*, 205.

176 Again, these symptoms are summarized from *Morrison, DSM-IV Made Easy*.

177 Letter to Bill Jacobs, 16 April 1931; see *A Vagabond for Beauty*, 39.

178 Everett Ruess Diary, 31 May 1932, in *Wilderness Journals*, 35.

179 Letter to Waldo, 12 July 1932; see *A Vagabond for Beauty*, 77–78.

180 Everett Ruess Diary, 18 July 1932, in *Wilderness Journals*, 67. "Have you never felt futility?" asks a character in a short story Everett wrote. "Have you never realized what a purposeless windmill life is?" ("The Bad Habit," n.d.).

181 Everett Ruess Diary, 21 July 1932, in *Wilderness Journals*, 71.

182 Ibid., 1 August 1933, in *Wilderness Journals*, 154.

183 Letter to Waldo, 11 August 1933, previously unpublished.

184 Everett Ruess Diary, 27 August 1933, in *Wilderness Journals*, 170.

185 Letter to Waldo, 29 November 1933, in "Youth Is for Adventure." The dating of this letter is problematic; earlier portions are reprinted in *A Vagabond for Beauty*, 151, which says that the addressee is unknown and dates it to May 1934.

186 Letter to Waldo, 22 December 1933; see *A Vagabond for Beauty*, 126–27.

187 Letter to Bill Jacobs, 17 June 1934; see *A Vagabond for Beauty*, 152–53.

188 Letter to Waldo, 2 May 1931; see *A Vagabond for Beauty*, 42–44.

189 Letter to Waldo, 12 July 1932; see *A Vagabond for Beauty*, 77–78.

190 Everett Ruess Diary, 6, 15, 29 September 1933, in *Wilderness Journals*, 179, 184, 200.

191 Portion of an untitled essay, quoted in letter to Edward Gardner, May 1934; see *A Vagabond for Beauty*, 148.

192 Letter to "addressee unknown," May 1934, in *A Vagabond for Beauty*, 151. According to "Youth Is for Adventure," however, portions of this letter were sent to Waldo from San Francisco and are dated 29 November 1933.

193 Letter to Bill Jacobs, 9 March 1931; see *A Vagabond for Beauty*, 32.

194 Letter to Bill Jacobs, 27–28 August 1931; see *A Vagabond for Beauty*, 57–58. See also Everett Ruess Diary, 1 July 1932, in *Wilderness Journals*, 54, as well as letter to Father, 18 August 1932: "[M]y ideals of friendship make it very difficult to find true friends" (in *A Vagabond for Beauty*, 86–87).

195 Everett Ruess Diary, 29 May 1932, in *Wilderness Journals*, 33.

196 Letter to Father, 27 January 1934; see *A Vagabond for Beauty*, 134.

197 Letter to Frances (surname unknown), 5 May 1934; see *A Vagabond for Beauty*, 145.

198 See Rusho's epilogue, as well as Everett Ruess Diary, 21 July 1932, in *Wilderness Journals*, 71. Additional references to Everett's health are found in a note from his parents and in his diary. His parents' note is appended to a typescript of Everett's essay "I Want to Go to Africa," written in 1928 when he was fourteen, which they included in "Youth Is for Adventure." They explained that the essay was originally part of "a letter of application to go with [an] expedition, [as] one of two [Boy] scouts, in Spring of 1928. Everett, however, on physical examination, was found to be barred by a temporary condition." Later in 1928 Everett recorded on 14 September: "The doctor is having me fast for 3 days, yesterday, today, tomorrow. Then I will be dieted." Three days later he added: "When I went to the doctors, Mr. McAllister checked over a list of my favorite foods and marked the ones I could eat, greatly decreasing my limitations. He also found that I had made a marked progress in chest development in the last week. Then he twisted me about & threw my legs up and spread my arms out, in ju jitsu style to loosen me up. He said I should have four small meals a day and be kept hungry."

199 See Jake Page, *Blood: The River of Life* (Washington, D.C.: U.S. News Books, 1981), 132–35.

200 *Johns Hopkins Symptoms and Remedies: The Complete Home Medical Reference* (New York: REBUS, 1995), 332.

201 Ibid.

202 The Columbia University College of Physicians and Surgeons, *Complete Home Medical Guide* (New York: Crown Publishers, 1985), 540.

203 *Everything You Need to Know about Diseases* (Springhouse, Pennsylvania: Springhouse Corporation, 1996), 593–94; Page, *Blood*, 133.

204 *The Johns Hopkins Medical Handbook: The 100 Major Medical Disorders of People Over the Age of 50* (New York: REBUS, 1992), 87.

205 See David E. Larson, ed., *Mayo Clinic Family Health Book*, 2nd ed. (New York: William Morrow and Company, Inc., 1996), 1064–65.

206 Taylor, *Sandstone Sunsets*, 93. Rusho may have also been alluding to Everett's sexual orientation when he wrote in 1983, "Everett Ruess was a highly complex young man with multiple consuming motivations we can only begin to understand. . . . That he may have concealed part of his nature even to his close friends and relatives is a possibility subject only to educated guesses" (*A Vagabond for Beauty*, viii; yet compare *Wilderness Journals*, 15).

207 Letter to Waldo, 12 July 1932; see *A Vagabond for Beauty*, 77.

208 Everett Ruess Diary, 1 July 1933, in *Wilderness Journals*, 127.

209 Letter to Waldo, 11 August 1933, previously unpublished.

210 Letter to Waldo, November 1934; see *A Vagabond for Beauty*, 178.

211 In *A Vagabond for Beauty*, 209.

212 Letter to Bill Jacobs, 10 May 1931; see *A Vagabond for Beauty*, 45.

213 Everett Ruess Diary, 23 May 1932, in *Wilderness Journals*, 28.

214 Ibid., 7–8 July 1932, in *Wilderness Journals*, 58.

215 Ibid., 28 May 1933, in *Wilderness Journals*, 95.

216 This is mistranscribed as "effeminately" in *A Vagabond for Beauty*, 77.

217 Everett's use of "queer" here may mean homosexual, although this is not certain.

218 Letter to Waldo, 12 July 1932; see *A Vagabond for Beauty*, 77.

219 Letter to Fritz Loeffler, 23 March 1933; see *A Vagabond for Beauty*, 95. Mark Taylor pointed out this intriguing exchange; see *Sandstone Sunsets*, 93–94.

220 Letter to Frances (surname unknown), 5 May 1934; see *A Vagabond for Beauty*, 145.

[221] Letter to Frances (surname unknown), May 1934; see *A Vagabond for Beauty*, 150.

[222] Everett Ruess Diary, 7 October 1933, in *Wilderness Journals*, 204.

[223] Ibid., 29 May 1932, in *Wilderness Journals*, 33. One of the last young men Everett spoke with before leaving Escalante remembered that he "never talked about any girlfriends, whether Navajo or otherwise" (in *A Vagabond for Beauty*, 208). Everett's concluding word in this last cited diary excerpt— "Obscurantism"—may be more revealing than he realized.

[224] Letter to Waldo, 22 December 1933; see *A Vagabond for Beauty*, 127.

[225] "Vultures," circa 1932–33, previously unpublished.

[226] The typescript has "mental anguish" here.

[227] These last two sentences are not in the typescript prepared by his parents.

[228] In another of Everett's unpublished stories, the main character is struck by a car and lies in a hospital bed, expecting to die. A friend pleads with him to live, but he answers, "What for?" turns away, and "weigh[s] certain thoughts in his mind." A week later, however, he has recovered and decided to live. "After all," he admits, "some bad habits are pleasant." ("The Bad Habit," n.d.) In yet a third unpublished story, "a solitary traveler" struggles through a storm to deliver an unspecified message. He sees a light in the distance. But "after a vain attempt to rise, he succumbed to his fate, and now he sleeps the eternal sleep of death." The next morning the inhabitants of the house he glimpsed find his body, "which testifie[s] to the triumph of Nature over Man. But the message he carried was never delivered." ("The Message," n.d.)

[229] "Portion of an essay" and Everett Ruess Diary, July 1932 (in *Wilderness Journals*, 72–73); and in *A Vagabond for Beauty*, 82–83.

[230] As he was leaving Escalante, Everett mailed home a batch—twenty, according to his mother— of watercolors to "lighten the load," as well as ten dollars. He had never before mailed money to his parents, but did so now because he "ha[d] more money than I need." "I want both of you to spend five for something you have been wishing to have—books, or a trip, but not anything connected with any kind of a duty," he wrote. "Let this be the first installment on that nickel I promised you when I made my first million" (letter to Father and Mother, 11 November 1934, in *A Vagabond for Beauty*, 176–77).

Often, the Navajo people grazed their sheep and goats in the canyons.

Bibliography

In addition to *Desert Magazine* and John Terrell's reports in the *Salt Lake Tribune* (see Appendix, pages 74–93), Everett Ruess's story has been recounted in a variety of publications, including the following:

Books

Abbey, Edward, author, and Philip Hyde, photographer. *Slickrock: The Canyon Country of Southeast Utah*. San Francisco: Sierra Club, 1971.

Henderson, Randall. *On Desert Trails Today and Yesterday*. Los Angeles: Westernlore Press, 1961.

Krakauer, Jon. *Into the Wild*. New York: Villard Books, 1996.

LeFevre, Lenora Hall, writer and compiler, and Nethella Griffin Woolsey, editor. *The Boulder Country and Its People: A History of the People of Boulder and the Surrounding Country, One Hundred Years, 1872–1973*. Springville, Utah: Art City Publishing, 1973.

On Desert Trails with Everett Ruess. With an introduction by Hugh Lacy and a foreword by Randall Henderson, editor, *Desert Magazine*. El Centro, California: Desert Magazine Press, 1940; 2nd ed., 1950.

Rusho, W. L. *Everett Ruess: A Vagabond for Beauty*. With an introduction by John Nichols and an afterword by Edward Abbey. Salt Lake City: Peregrine Smith Books [Gibbs Smith, Publisher], 1983.

———, editor. *Wilderness Journals of Everett Ruess*. Salt Lake City: Gibbs Smith, Publisher, 1998.

Shoumatoff, Alex. *Legends of the American Desert: Sojourns in the Greater Southwest*. New York: Alfred A. Knopf, 1997.

Smith, Gibbs. "Everett Ruess." In *Utah History Encyclopedia*, edited by Allan Kent Powell. Salt Lake City: University of Utah, 1994.

Stegner, Wallace. *Mormon Country*. New York: Duell, Sloan and Pearce, 1942.

Taylor, Mark A. *Sandstone Sunsets: In Search of Everett Ruess*. Salt Lake City: Gibbs Smith, Publisher, 1997.

Topping, Gary. *Glen Canyon and the San Juan County*. Moscow: University of Idaho Press, 1997.

Documentary

[Taylor, Dyanna.] *Vanished!* Turner Broadcasting System (aired 13 January 1999).

Magazines, Newspapers, and Periodicals

Banks, Leo W. "Wandering Soul," *Tucson Weekly* (8–14 May 1997).

Boren, Ray. "A Legend Lingers: Was Young Writer Murdered 65 Years Ago in Wilderness?" *Deseret News* (2 May 1999).

Church, Lisa. "Ruess Mystery Haunts Canyon Country," *Salt Lake Tribune* (24 May 1999).

Fish, Peter. "The Legend of Everett Ruess: The Escalante Trail," *Sunset Magazine* (February 1997).

Kehmeier, G. C. "What Happened to Everett Ruess?" *Trail and Timberline* (April 1966).

Leadabrand, Russ. "Desert Mystery," *Pasadena Independent* (21 November 1955).

Leap, Norris. "Utah Canyons Veil Fate of L.A. Poet," *Los Angeles Times* (15 June 1952).

Mitchell, Riley. "Everett Ruess Exhibit at Atrium Gallery," *The Catalyst* (October–November 1987).

Roberts, David. "What Happened to Everett Ruess?" *National Geographic Adventure* (Spring 1999).

Schindler, Harold. "Explorers, Vagabonds Added to Lore of New National Monument," *Salt Lake Tribune* (22 September 1996).

Scholl, Barry. "In Search of Everett Ruess: An Enduring Legend," *Salt Lake City* magazine (November–December 1996).

List of Illustrations

Blockprints

by Everett Ruess

Happy Journeys! front cover
Monument Valley, cover, 48
Untitled [buttes], 1
Granite Towers, 3
Sea Spire, 6
Sky Seekers, 10
Battlements of the Colorado, 14
Untitled. "My little dog Curly, Cynthia, Percival, and I," 16
Canyon del Muerto, 20
Square Tower House, Mesa Verde, Colorado, 22
Granite and Cypress, 28
Mountain Shadows, 34
Tsegi Canyon, 47
Untitled [leafless tree], 59
Wild Coastline, 69
Tomales Bay, Fishing Shack, 73
Untitled [fence and rocks], 97

Maps

by Norton Allen
Where Everett Ruess Vanished . . . , xiv
by the *Salt Lake Tribune* staff
Route of the *Salt Lake Tribune*'s 1935 Expedition in Search of Everett Ruess, 79
by the Gibbs Smith, Publisher, staff
Everett Ruess Country, 98

Photographs

by Everett Ruess
"Cloudbanks arched everywhere overhead, . . . ," 13
Everett's burros, descending "mountain trails between white-mantled pines," 17
"The water . . . is roaring out like a maelstrom, whipping itself to froth . . . ," 18
"Square Tower House, Mesa Verde, Colorado," 22
Shiprock, Navajo Reservation, New Mexico, rising like "a ghostly galleon in a sea of sand," 36
Errant burros, enjoying "an extra ration of oats," 38
Wily burros, choosing "to bed down in that little hogan," 43
Fascinating ruins, "dating from eight hundred to 15 hundred years back," 50
Sleepy burro, taking it easy during the heat of the day, 56
Curly, taking a much-needed break, 71
"There are . . . only [a few places] . . . where a man might camp. Man camps only at water," 93
". . . we learned of the many cliff dwellings [Everett] had seen, and of his precarious climbs to some high isolated ones," 116
Often, the Navajo people grazed their sheep and goats in the canyons, 127
"Strange sad winds roared down the canyon, roaring [through the trees] . . . ," 130
by Tad Nichols
Everett and Randolph Jenks, loading Ruess's burro into the back of the pick-up truck, 61

by Wes Visel
    Everett and friends, getting "an early start," 31
by Others
    Everett Ruess and his dog, Curly, ii
    Everett and Curly, relaxing at home in Los Angeles, 1931, x
    Everett and friends, preparing to "take the trail again in a few days," 8
    Everett, Nuflo, and Jonathan, pausing in Canyon de Chelly, Arizona, 1932, 25
    Everett, taking a moment to relax, 105

Watercolor

by Everett Ruess
    On and On and On! xiii

"Strange sad winds roared down the canyon,
roaring [through the trees] . . ."

Gary James Bergera has been associated as a writer and/or editor with *Dialogue, Journal of Mormon History, Sunstone, Utah Historical Quarterly,* and the *Utah History Encyclopedia.* He lives and works in Salt Lake City.

W. L. Rusho is an editor *(Everett Ruess: A Vagabond for Beauty* and *Wilderness Journals of Everett Ruess)* and writer *(Lee's Ferry—Desert River Crossing* and *Powell's Canyon Voyage)* who resides in Salt Lake City.